design psychology

Towards a definition of design

TABLE OF CONTENTS

Prologue - The Long Curious Night

For the last fifteen years along looking into a posing question my research has led me in an intriguing direction. Firstly it was purely one of psychology, it was – 'where is the architectural theory of human biology'? Perhaps a fruitless question, it mostly led to dry results, those I could do very little with.

Over my following steps came perhaps the turn of events I was looking for. This came deeper within my career as a designer, much deeper. I found the shoe was quite literally on the other foot, and I discovered the mirror image of my earlier endeavors. Slowly it posed itself into yes – a question. This one was along the lines of 'what is the spirit or soul of design'?

How could it be that I had graduated design school, especially having formerly been a huge fanatic of psychology, and entirely missed the understanding of the theory of people in design? How could I have been so absent in my overall thinking and attention. In a sense this guilt spurred me along the direction that led to writing the contents of this book.

Placing myself back under my research 'hat' and getting back to where it all began. There was a slow material trail of what I was seeking to answer. Along this path there were fascinating components that all seemingly had aspects of Art, Design & Psychology that left me needing fulfillment and tangible answers. These would have to be the kind of answers that could be plugged into the big picture – even philosophically. Not only this but there would have to be equal plug-ins to the hard practices & methodologies that were within design school. All of this without the betrayal of the central and well worked out theories of Psychology itself.

If there is room to say, I have to add that this was a fulfilling line of query and came to perhaps the most wonderful answers of my research and curious academic life, becoming the fruits of my looking. Now, when I go through my day I have these pieces of my research comforting my very thoughts about how Design & Psychology are inter-twinned.

Without a doubt, this is a book for people who hold a love for design. In this way it is also a book for anyone discovering Psychology, and just wants some answers to the relationships people have had with human creativity.

To place these 2 questions together has yielded a whole line of questions that have enriched my life and hopefully it makes any reader smile with satisfaction of how this book works its way through their answers. In the big picture there are ideas, there are concepts, there are harmonious relationships, and then there is the obvious. We shall explore a little bit of each in our search for balance. In it we will come to many other intriguing questions and without delay there are answers, quick to fulfill our curiosity.

Imagination it seems is much more tangible and real than we are led to believe. Actually sitting here with pen, paper and coffee, under electric lights in an urban setting is all the proof one requires to see what humans are made of. Otherwise we would still be without spear – eating plants out in the fringes of some be gone forest some place – cowering mostly. It is obvious we crossed that line so far back that nobody has even a sniff about when it actually happened, and who really cares? It certainly did happen, and as the saying goes there is little looking back for most people. Progress as ingenuity is wonderful – it is so human – but, what is it? And where the heck does it come from?

Which leads us to one of the biggest questions – 'why'?

Maybe the answer is obvious, but have you ever tried to write it down so that it isn't a rambling mess? Why did humans dig themselves out of the grass, and how is a modern creative human a solid relative of the distant creative human? This is a legitimate question, at least in my mind, so I set out to answer it.

What I discovered is that curiosity is one of the most potent drivers of a person, and there you have a piece of the answer - curiosity. It is almost an irritating craving to deal with. It's not like you can just get a bite to eat and your hankering to know dissipates. This is how perhaps imagination starts to mix in the human brain. But what does this say about creativity, what of the artist? What does the posing question indicate of cave painters? Clearly Design should have something to say about this.

One needs to become agile in the art of stepping back and looking at the puzzle from a nice vantage point, out where you can see where something begins and yet also where it ends. Further along the line my studies seemed to be peeling away at the pieces that are best explained as the social context of design. Just what is design's stance on social and societal development? Indeed I wanted to know, so I looked and found usually very little except for other professionals with a similar question of what does design have to say about the human culture it so helps to create? It seems allot of folks want to know.

Perhaps, just maybe while I was in school I didn't just simply snooze my way through those important lectures where the answers had been so apply provided. Perhaps just maybe they were never mentioned and never said.

There it is, the journey, the long winding road that brought me peace and so many answers to ongoing questions, alas. It has become a comfortable place, my new vantage point on the subjects of design & psychology, felt out much the same way as any useful product is- chaotically.

It has become a big-idea answer, not fitting neatly into any simple boxes, instead appeared a more serious frame. It came along one of my long-held suspicions, that maybe this is not even a problem of the linear sort but one existing outside of norm. To digest any useful answers here a person has to cross over from that oh so comfortable perch in the land of static parameters and pass over into the land of the wandering constants. That is, in my mind, what has made defining the scope of the 'designing human' more attainable, because not humans, reality, nor design are linear things. It is kind of a lump we all have to swallow. It will require a twist of the mind to see the simplicity.

The world which we were raised in is the land of the fluid variable. To get cleanly through this one needs a method to apply within the idea. It requires visualization of the first designers to ever walk the grassy fields in search of future.

Design is human, that is the bold end result. To understand a hand full of items of ourselves is to clearly see what design is – an action, a characteristic habit. But it isn't just that simple. We are dealing with a complex beast, both in ourselves and in our own understanding of nature. This is part of the aspect that design as a practice is itself looking for.

"To be human a man must understand what has been accomplished and what can be accomplished by the arts of man"

Richard McKeon

Indeed what we are doing here is a bargain of an adventure, and we shall go far in its discovery and things possible yet. Searching out the very nature of design is a bit like tracking a wild animal, it could be anywhere, but probably isn't. How shall we go about it? Should we head towards the bastion of quantitative thoughts, and just offer a canned answer? Or shall we send for the depths of organized hell and launch straight into the unknown abyss of chaos, where we may come unglued and overdose on experimental ideas?

To be at all certain of where we are going we sort of have to know history. In some of my readings I came across a sort of piece of knowledge, I had to articulate it myself. It said that post-modern art is an art form that while criticizing history it aspires to nothing containing future. This in what I gathered it to mean was rather vexing, and sort of a hyperbole in itself. While being an invention it implies why shall we bother to invent anything from here on in? It's a sort of trick, but it contains brutal inflections about our human state. Whether I was right or terribly mistaken in my deductions I wanted to see well past it. So I looked into some deep history instead, into the first known things, and it became a trip and a half. There is a saying, to understand a person one needs to walk a mile in their shoes. Well, I sort of wanted to walk a mile, or a half a mile anyway, in the shoes (bare feet?) of a cave dweller. Just to know what they were thinking. Oh my, what a daunting task they faced, what impossible odds of getting to where people complain about having slow internet. It is a strange brew of thoughts to hold. What kind of a future they had to face, and we are here today, so obviously they made it. It is a startling thought, because they are our ancestors, and in many ways they are us, but without anything yet done. They had to put their hardest faces on and move forward. It is a thought and a half. I doubt many people now days would be up to the task.

More or less that is the kind of place that we shall visit in this process of a book. This was the mental experiment that I went through in putting this edition together over the last decade and a half.

This book deals with design on a human level and within our human experience. It will cover a sort of line of thinking through many topics and shall wander through the human mind as well as ideas about the human brain and natural networks in order to define design. So if you like settle in and get comfy.

Better Thinking, Therefore Design

Knowledge, it can be said, is the driver of all progress. We build our understanding upon the foundations laid before us, from those that were before us, with the intention to keep going even when the path is not well lit.

Giving a quality to a field of knowledge, let's say geometry, usually means that there are well defined boundaries to where it fits within its parent discipline, that in this case being mathematics. All in all this is a straight forward aspect. Psychology, as a relatively young discipline of study has earned its appropriate credibility from its time spent chiseling out its boundaries, what is as well as what isn't within the scope of its borders. Add to this its tests under fire of criticism, and its survival as a study, as an art. The thing is design, isn't quite like this. A messier series of channels spatter its identity upon an area or 2, it is an extremely difficult thing to place into the previously mentioned quality. The thing is we haven't done it yet, and from the present appearance of things we aren't even that close to doing so.

Is it worth our time to go into perhaps clarifying, making its relationship to all that we see design as being and equally apparent to any single participant? Can we clearly explain exactly what design is in a short simple way? Why not, after all what is more human than designing things, isn't it the calling card of mankind, we who have thumbs?

Expressing design as an art seems to be the apparent path. In this we can freely express how it fits in with the general studies of Universities, as well as being aware of just what it is and just what it is not. With the knowledge of seeing design as an art we will be able to demonstrate how it fits in with the bigger picture of what we already know.

There seem to be 2 outstanding characteristics of design. The first is that it is the development of the means to affect one's surroundings, or something near to this. The second is that, in every which way you approach design it seems to be a sort of applied vision. Sadly though, these are local responses to a global question. To fracture them one only needs to ask the question 'why'? In this way these are not intellectual definitions of something that is so visible to every single human that design can be many things all at once. Knowledge has to be based within the big picture.

If I were to be a visitor from another galaxy, lost within a large art gallery, wondering, and finally asked some other individual 'what does it all mean?', the chances are I will get a good explanation as to what paintings are and the value they give. Now if I were the same Martian, lost in a museum of old technology, do you think I could get such a definitive and highly influential response? The answer is no, because we aren't totally sure ourselves. We don't actually have a formal theory worked out. Highly fragmented islands of such things are easy, but they are not ubiquitous. Often these ideas are sheltered within technical descriptions or amongst consumer notions. Nothing is linked the way it should be and conversations need to relate to other conversations on the same topic, it requires more rudder.

And what does knowledge have to do with people, very much allot, but not really in the eyes of a definition of design as it now exists. In a sense psychology has worked this out, such as people are highly complex and knowledge can be internal as well as external, as in society. It can reside in the brain and within our self-awareness, or even the conscious or the sub-conscious. That is where the discipline has earned its stripes, in being definitive in its self.

The Wild Card

Counter to most theories is control. To imagine that prediction is possible in the real world is highly myopic. What this tenders is that variability is highly variable. People as well as the world we help compose are so complex that even the most sophisticated algorithms are no match for explaining anything but models.

What does this have to do with people, what does this have to do with design? The short reply is, well, everything. Everything imaginable, plus more, simply due to the fact that people must live within the world and design must live within people and this world, so both are exceptionally complicated. Thus there is no floating modern day way of summing up design.

Floating parameters, in this sense, are what we shall label the container that design exists in, if it were to be summarized and simplified. The field is constantly changing, the positions of the players and the pieces are never the same twice and time is a hindrance. Welcome to the reality, the theatre, where a definition of design must be born.

In a sense we can call it the non-linear theatre, and there

is no way around it. Just as people have to live here, so do their products. This is one of the differences between facts & knowledge. Facts are fixed and redundant, and knowledge is highly malleable. This is what makes knowledge a tool, and to the user, their best chance to measure the chaos of the floating parameters. Patterns, one must find the inner workings of all present goings on, to glean out the ideas that will persist well after all the shapes have shifted upon the board.

This is the easy explanation as to why design has no foundation as a liberal art, too many things are not yet begun. There has existed genius after genius in the various fields of design, all seemed to have lived mainly on local islands of expertise and understanding. This part is without doubt. With so much confined wisdom there has been little to compose what might be considered an education in the big relationship that people and products play, meaning across the entire field.

The item most valuable here is that design is non-linear, just as people are. There is no other way. To explain it as a body of knowledge this must be accepted and followed, for the wisdom lay within.

The Wandering Path

This in itself is probably the most important concept to digest in order to get to our desired point of knowing. In metaphorical sense, design is like a river. This river is composed of an overwhelming number of drops of water, just as in human history each person would be each drop, we will never know how many of us have ever existed, not even close. Within the wandering river, there is force, this represents the trends and force of all the people living on earth at any mark of time. Also the surface is on an infinite bed of sand, which it tosses and turns upon given the force and water affecting the exact path. These grains of sand represent universe variables, and sometimes the river is connected to some and only some of the grains. The grains affect the river, they affect each other. Along the way of the river there are ponds, small ones mostly. It is here where we define something. A pond is a small and real pool of water that happens temporarily. Water (people) go in and out of the ponds if they can. Within a pond is a localized methodology. It is a metaphor of a temporary use of an invention used by the people, it comes and later it disappears.

More or less the idea to draw from this analogy is that Design as knowledge is like the river, you cannot see where it dips into the horizon, and it carries the people along with it, along the sand as it travels through time. Along its way some designs are a diversion. What this is separating for us is that Design and designs are not the same concept. Knowledge is to be found explaining the river, not the pools. The pools are only technical. The river is the wisdom, and wisdom is what we seek. Design is not linear, it is a wondering path.

Social Knowledge

Any solid definition for design must be fully tied in with social systems, as it is the only reason for the existence of design itself. As a social entity can be any number of people, there is no way to separate people and the act of designing, they are forever tied together.

In this we see that there is a long line of people that have come before us, with their designs. This is obvious, and as such is integral to explaining what design is by including the ancient past, the present as well as the future. Being part of such scope of people is in a way being part of the study being analyzed here, and just as cave paintings exist too does the need to include those artists in any real outcome.

An effectiveness of communication has to be central with what was composed in these ancient paintings, after all we found them and deciphered much of their content. It must be this quality for a definition to purvey much more than products, the paintings are so much more than ink.

Over a lifetime of some object being employed by people, let's say televisions, there comes an understanding amongst everyone. In several ways it is manifested, maybe like culture, and to people who are aware of all that is television, that life without it would be & had been different. This is a social network of change, and it is the type that Design should be able to confidently and cleanly explain. After all we are simply talking about an electronic product, but really we are getting into the behaviour and the resulting mindset which follows it use. This is somewhat unknowable before it happens, but should fit into a framework that does acknowledge its affect taking place.

Designers should refine that they are 'culture-shapers', often more so than they are merely technicians. As a study this is rather central. It is about social effects as well as the nature of action + behaviour of   culture on the receiving end.

Artists need theory that includes social outcomes, with a human-centric theme. Designers within their needs for knowledge certainty require much qualitative communication amongst any society. A connection between the workings of design – and the individual grasping it, this should be the same for the small group as well as for a complex society. It is the hallmark of a comprehensive idea of the profession, one which leaves the room with confidence in its creativity and psychology within its heart. In this way there is simplicity enough for complexity in its definition.

Clarity of understanding must be there so that each person in a discussion of the idea is on the same page, whether they are within related or distant fields of expertise. Short and clear in each perception of the global topic and how it is internally related to facets of the profession throughout.

In an effort to further expose the meaning of this direction, let us employ a model. In a way it will serve as a filter, someone may be able to process a question through the model. **

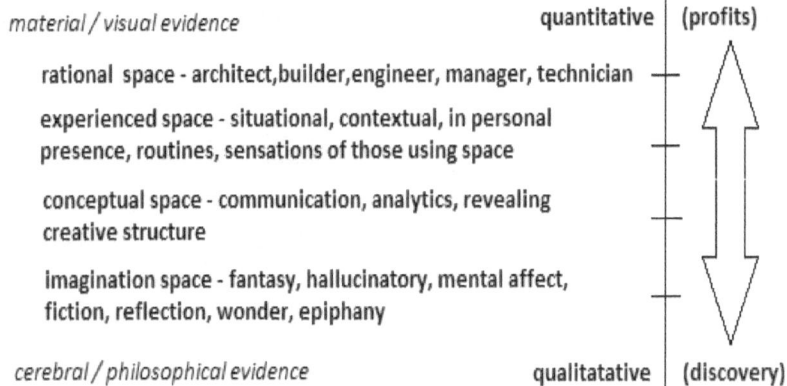

material / visual evidence   quantitative | (profits)

rational space - architect,builder,engineer, manager, technician

experienced space - situational, contextual, in personal
presence, routines, sensations of those using space

conceptual space - communication, analytics, revealing
creative structure

imagination space - fantasy, hallucinatory, mental affect,
fiction, reflection, wonder, epiphany

cerebral / philosophical evidence   qualitatative | (discovery)

Fig A: The Umbrella Model **

>   *******This model uses some associations developed by Larissa
Fassler, Martin Heidegger & Helene Furjan*

The model is meant to clear up just what kind of players
there are within the overall process of design. If we know
who is in the field all at once we can begin to take it all in
and at once describe what relationships are there. This
model exists for past, present & future aspects. The types
of questions someone can run through the model would
be, 'where does an artistic person fit in with the material
products made?' Or 'what does the average citizen have
to do with design anyway?' Another example would be
'does a technician exist on an island free of design
creation?'

The objective of the Umbrella Model is to express
openness and inclusion to the list of players involved in
the process. It shall help us discern a proper final

definition for design. It is a social analysis for us to play with and form connections. Links need study to develop answers.

After all, what we are attempting to do is find the relationships between societies and initial creativity, wherever that creativity begins to spark. When we find the network our view will improve.

A Clear Definition

People make things what they are, as in what meaning becomes attached to them. In this sense you will not even gain the same answers from different groups. People are difficult, clustering and almost impossible to comprehend. Something you think is going to happen won't, and something that shouldn't take place does. It's just the way behaviour flows. It begins in one place and ends in another.

Keeping track of the variables you can comprehend is enough of a task. For someone looking to alter groups of people with intent, there becomes much interference in a short amount of time. It is more an idea than an actual practice. One can name perhaps a hundred inventions that should not be in use, and a hundred more that should be. It is all part of the heavily psychological field. Experts do what they can, but design is more of a life form than a job.

The truth is that design can easily eat entire civilizations, out of control ideas, competing armies, bad agricultural tactics. Same coin flip side, it can make societies out of very thin air, as we shall explore later. Anyone who doesn't think they have any skin in this game is likely mistaken, design includes every person on earth. You wear a shoe today? Walk on a road? Yup you're in it.

Here is the thing, it is very slippery. It almost veers for no man, but at the same time is of man. It is as mentioned – a beast. Our understanding has to reflect this awareness.

Design is much more than 'craft', just as a car is much more than a mode of transportation. To take in the surrounding possibilities and relationships at work is to give true solidity. To attempt to congeal some of the inherent social complexity at work is to make progress here. Initial understanding can be either on the side of the creators, or the side of the users of items digested. Where we firm up exactly the universal matter will come later as we explore.

In such we are dealing with the realm of art & psychology, meaning it cannot be simply a static description, objectivity just isn't the idea. As such, products are not an explanation of the design process, just as paintings are not so much about paint being applied to things. An active definition is what we seek, it is more of a comprehension of what people are involved in than solving small problems singularly. The discovery process is extremely vital to seeing this definition as a whole.

"Design is any proactive behaviour which correlates mental imagery to the physical, in an effort to cause lasting effect."
(Michael Gronnerud)

This as a definition is what we are going with for the entirety of this edition. Lying within it will be open plug-ins for each of the criteria we have discussed. This definition requires some thought. It is both simple and yet incredibly versatile. It is both specific and yet accepting of the floating parameters. It has conformity with our non-linear choice, and it is fungible to fit the scopes of opposing design thinking. For now this is our vantage point, and within the following sequences of question & answer we shall test it, to see if we come out the other side with all limbs attached. We can have something here, a vehicle perhaps, in which to properly see the beast from a comfortable position. All good stories have a beginning, perhaps this is it for our knowledge of a definition of design.

PART I

THE DESIGN MIND

Not knowing something, is what makes something worth knowing...which makes it worth figuring out...which is where we come in...humans....that's rather what we do, it's rather our style. Design is about the aggregate of some things....ideas & object's functionality....and it is as well a style, where we together get to form a story about ourselves. From this we get meaning. This also gives us balance, for humans are nothing if not what we make with our hands our emotions and our minds. This gives us both place and purpose in this world, and it certainly gets our collective attention. Upon this after much specialization comes a certain sophistication. This has been demonstrated to become infectious, with our interpretations and with its impressions. Invention is our very own interpretation of what nature has given us to work with and of what we've made with it says volumes...about ourselves.

Preface–
A Little Something Known as Deep Design

When we get into the topic of people we tend to have ideas, about what we are, where we are coming from and where is it that we want to go. Within the conversation it is seemingly impossible to get very far in without broaching the ever popular topic of design.

Within ourselves exists much mystery and with a strong sense of self and an impression of potential we gift ourselves into the creative pursuits that are the arts. Along-side these styles of representation and outlets of self-awareness comes another brash endeavor, that of tool making. You have it separate, as if in the hand different aspects of a cube, one expressive to the greatest potential and the other the highway to deliver us to that expression. The means to make our way through a task there has always been the tool kit. And without our deep roots in carving stone there would be still no foundation to lay all of our technology and creativity upon. This is our basis of all that is Deep Design. How did we get here and where in our ancestors minds did the first bolts of light come striking forth?

These are in fact monster sized questions, in all practicality we will never know the full truth, but through collective analogy and observation of bits left over from our ancient selves we can piece together a very tangible likelihood of how it all gradually unfolded. There is a bread crumb trail there if we have the will to follow it into our own past, and into ourselves. This is the basis of the creative mind that has always been present.

Why is it that we want to design in the first place? Is it that there really can be some sort of positional answer? What is it in us that leads us to visualize in the first place, and what spry motivation is priming us to create things with our hands? This is a curiosity indeed and it is also a mirror onto our very selves.

For how long has this nature taken residence within us? Is it purely artistic for the sake of being fancy or expressive, or is it something stirring deeper? Has it boiled up within us only in the last several centuries, or millennia, or far longer, how will we ever find out? Can time even be part of the equation, or is it more along the lines of this is being human at any point in time? Is this state one that is carnal, or innate, or emotionally charged and thereby attached to whatever it is just to be human? With these questions just what exactly are we stumbling onto, how big are the perimeters of these questions?

This book explores deeper into the foundations of design and shows some of the linkages within our old selves along with the modern aspects of how we live with and currently think about design. It is something so absolutely central to our existence, as if it is a key to what problems are and the path we choose to take to gain solutions. Taking a journey well across the border of the obvious and reflecting back something of ourselves is just what Deep Design attempts to do, to lay out and examine what we know and what lines can be drawn where we consider design as part of our lives. Just as the stirring within us makes us curious, it also leads us into making things that leave us just as curious, it is central to the human condition.

3

The seemingly simple act of shaping an item from raw resource is still different from what can be called a design school or a variant. Designers, have to be knowledgeable of just how creative results fit into a larger trend, these modern days we are aware of the types of purposes that lay within their work and all too aware of how tools and technologies shape our lives, even when they are invisible. We look towards something more subtle, it is the raw craft that is primary to this pursuit. An item with function but without bias of methods, it is a pure item which we can devise or distill out of thin air. Just as the first fishing net or protective glove would have been devised, in such distant times there was an urge to create them.

Where can we begin, where can we have an initial witnessing of all the later cohesion? When will we first see it in the human time line, an almost abstract concept here but one that rests solidly in the physical world? Items fitting into groups or into styles would tend to grasp this initial concept. This entails much of the modern definition of design as it likely exists for most of us, it represents the kernel of basis to all the wonderful stuff we now surround ourselves in and fill our homes with.

Art, sculpture, craft, design & architecture, these will all seem archetypes, like containers, separating all the beginnings and growth of ideas, to reveal beginnings. These will become real and tangible as the tree of ideas seems to grow out of design in general.

All good paths must start with a good question, all fascination must begin with an unknown, this is what characterizes first steps.

Introduction–
The Humble Beginnings

Gaining meaning from something usually means piling a large amount of ourselves into its pursuit. Usually by putting a lot of time into that something then that meaning is manually brought to light. Endlessly investing into discovery, that of invention, that of bringing it along takes time and energy. This requires what only humans can do, it is by getting the inner truth out of objects, rather than just sitting in our caves all day and watching wild beasts go by.

It is in us to be captivated, to be enthralled about something, to become creative & to settle out what we abstractly perceive things to be like, or even what they could be. It is with consideration that we place ourselves so deeply into some act or some art, to get into what it is to become, before it itself can then be. Before the tools that we adore become a part of our everyday lives we must first place them there, we must first invent them into being right there in front of us. This has a lot to do with what a human being is in fact about. We love to explore things, to wonder, to be curious about many things which may in fact resemble each other if we choose to interact with our physically surroundings. From the very first story, people went out and made possibilities, after that there was no looking back, the compass had been forever turned.

Further into our casting of items, into some physical manipulation of objects, with it came the development of the alphabet, or the making of the wheel, first it took a daunting investment of time & effort, all seemingly so obvious and worth it to us now. But these things were not ever thus, they had to be milled out of thin air, shaped out of rock, etched out of our minds, out of the oblivion itself. It took a certain 'leap of self-placement', forever putting us out there, into our surroundings, in order to grasp the very concept it is, that of cause & effect and ourselves. It is the very idea that we can modify things, even if they seem forever out of sight in the beginning.

Learning to Mold

Whatever it is, this human tenacity, in its own right, how does it allow us to inject our minds into a problem? However does it allow us to project the roles involved in play, those in the field of activity? It, this very persistence, gives us the simplistic eyesight to partake into whatever exploring may be at hand as we attempt to investigate our desired result, as we take the first blind steps out of the dark. If even that is as simple as having the ability to make fire, or then again make fire anytime we want. This is, as a notion, a very high concept even if it is simple.

The thoughtful consideration behind the possibility itself is to make something firmly possible, is this more like what we have gone after with our time? This is the pragmatic visual field that is a central part of what it is to be human, to solve things, to apply ourselves with a definition of what is it we are actually doing. Some living creatures are just better at modification than others, but this is thinking, this is something else, this is altogether different.

It is substantially more than some consideration, in

spending the time to make things more than into an aspect of style. What is style on its own anyway? Solidly an idea must follow a honing, a refinement, an obsession, that of making things better, until eventually it gains a life of its own, into something identifiably itself. What is the point of style then, if only adding to some functionality? Could it be on a level with sophistication and towards a level of perception? To utilize any tool is to grasp and embody the core of insight itself, by adding something novel to something else known, well that is the specific use of perception. To use materials to gain a toe-hold, to gain some ability, to achieve some know-how, and to foster knowledge, this is where people can grasp further potential. This is the clever human. This is the sophistication. It is an act of self-determination.

Once a living being has made the choice to adapt an object and to manipulate it to further alter their lives, the decision has been made to cross the bridge into a certain type of world of intrigue and intelligence and never look back.

Design ... is of mind, & only a mind can design unknown things.

The question becomes then, did any particular ideas have a psychological impact upon a society, around the adaptation of normal or otherwise boring neighborhood materials? If this is the case then it seems a clear episode of design and the impact of altering the potential of strategic materials. The capacity to shape, the ability to rethink, the desire to visualize and the changing of a body of material around present need becomes the very root of production all at once. This leads us to ask, did the first craftsmen stumble accidentally onto the idea of mass production?

How and when in societal groups did craftsmen have the direction to alter the path of those who share their community. By providing tools to a village things would undergo a major evolution. A population being given the power of their first sets of tools would possibly be as important for the future potential of the group as any other social change.

Technical knowledge.... one could make the argument, that a monkey has some level of 'technical achievement' as long as they use shaped stones as tools for then they crack nuts for nutrition. This is a paradigm shift when humanoids took up the challenge and got specific with those stones. The underlying reflection is telling us that some monkeys have learned how the fabrication of a tool results in a better life, they have at least this intentionality, they have made the very first step.

The ability to shape the world around them requires this first untethered leap, that of manipulating the present materials. It is here, in the moment of first inception where the idea overtook the environmental landscape, for good practices of design were born.

Exactly what is it then that pushed the individual mind into this position & kept it there?

Learning of the process, learning of the technique required to form useful and consistent tools. The stone forming as well, that was relayed back to the carver from the stone. This is the two way exchange of knowledge and information made in a session of carving for the human, a ubiquitous tutorial from the patterns within the stones themselves and on the possibilities of rocks and their usefulness. Getting into this process of consistency would have become a honing of thought altogether. The known ordeal of carving would have been transforming itself as the learning to pay some attention progressed. The rock, in many ways, became the teacher and the details become the lesson.

The details within would have become the prize, and the human brain the cavity in which to store such gems of information. How magnificent it would have been to base today's work upon yesterday's lessons.

Chapter One–
It All Began by a Lake

> *This has everything to do with the function of society...*

Tools you say, just some items of modern man for the most part, how about with a few ancient exceptions to that tone. After all what would cave dwellers be doing with tools? If we had a window to the ancient beginnings of when and perhaps where this all began to take place the South of Africa would be that. Even with where ancient tool crafting had all its first action is in fact available to us, and it certainly will tell us so much more about the individuals who were up to this curious practice.

In a very retroactive sort of sense this is a high grade insight. Archeologists have the physical evidence which portrays the mental aptitudes going at the time at specific locations. Can men you say, be forgiven for living in caves, if it could be shown that it was they who began this crazy endeavor into invention itself, would this be a fair conclusion?

Only as recent as July 2011 (Sonia Harmand, Jason Lewis – Stoney Brook University) a question became posed as to whom exactly was responsible for crafting a lot of tools, the kind that were arguably non-existent, and the kind that would never be found. This is when they came to be absolutely tangible.

That is after they were dug up in Kenya on the shores of

Lake Turkana. Stone tools made for single purposes. It became likely that they were highly specific instruments, and were carved and assembled by individuals who knew one another. Still intact and verifiable by archeologists when they were found was the understanding of what they had uncovered. It adds to a list of previous discoveries of hand-made tools, just the fact that these are many hundreds of thousands of years old, this particular batch (150 tools) is referred to as the LOM3 artifacts.

These things are incidental. There is little chance of ever discovering a batch of items this old, and yet the possibilities still exist. In a sense this may lend to the idea that there were enough items out there that at some point some fraction of there ever happening would be brought into the light.

It is just that it has happened more than once that a batch of crafted items has made its way back into our hands, bringing with it a diary of sorts. Whether we are talking about the act of making the tools or their later discovery, in actuality proves the same point. As we now know there were many upon many thousands of African axes, each hand made over some reasonable amount of years, and over the span of many millennia.

It is an unavoidable concept that time was to reveal the density of the trend of shaping stones and for practical uses it had been a very common occurrence hundreds of thousands of years ago. It was happening at a certain enough rate to illustrate for archeologists that the choices of stone shapers was to continue along this path, to form items was to better their quality of life. Further forming the tools into shapes like axes was simply a matter of time.

Without the physical evidence these ideas would be fringing on the world of the abstract. This means that the concepts of time & development would have to be rooting into the unknowable mind of the craftsman. But this is not the case, as the items have shown what a good use of time the crafting indeed was, even so long ago.

These would serve psychologically beyond the use of the tools and as a marker of the larger picture, that which noted a sea change in the thinking of hunter-gatherer society. Hammers & axes were carved and they were the way forward as well as a meaningful practice to produce on a large scale. It was a life enhancing technology, that which bettered the daily routines of their makers. It demonstrates a type of division of labour, of specialized practices within groups. With so much work to do some sect became better at the production of tools than others, and viola.!

The implications of this are quite staggering. From the grasping of how to go about the design of the tools and the allowance of resources, all the way to a factory-like settings.

This raw perspective, buried deep in the mind of those who made the tools, became rather mind-altering. Here the stone was demonstrating its power to the carver, nature as teacher, carver as student. Here we have already answered our first question, 'why design', well it was obvious even to a cavemen. The path became chosen very early on and this is where we all got started. In the specifics of what all was happening while these tools were being formed on the banks of Lake Turkana we have little way of defining generalities of life, but it is apparent that the drive was born from within the groups themselves.

People, or ancient man, designed against the odds, pushing against failure, against the prospect that it is a complete waste of one's time. It had become done either way, and it was done because the benefits far outweighed the costs.

Deep Design

Is it then that this ancient version of a tool maker represents Deep Design? What would this imply about modern man and all we consider to be design, in a contemporary sense? A way of thinking, that which takes the evidence into consideration is required because we would like to know the intentions of craftsmanship.

Attention to detail has existed past ourselves as modern humans, back far into our roots. It is an analysis of the environmental and our own psychological floor that lies within design sense or design functionalism. An actual need to alter things around us has been taking place for hundreds of thousands of years.

The layers with the practice itself reveal what is this perspective on making stuff out of stone, when the need to do so was never obvious before it happened.

The practice of design is complex, and what drives it forward and where it shows us to be in a modern sense, within a design environment working with raw things there must exist intention.

To establish some route of considering ideas like these, into some style of reference, this deep design notion is about promoting our rooting of creativity. In many forms it becomes a batch of our own collective stories, those showing where we came from. In another form it is an envelope of thinking, that which considers just what is going on when the spark of need meets that of forming tools, or chairs or ever more sophisticated items.

It gradually forms a picture, a fabric that is qualitative, which is the utmost beam which design psychology must rest upon. It is in fact a story, one that relates much too human desire, our own cause and effect, as to creative forces dwelling within our ideas.

How much did all of this pounding of rocks bring 'people' together? How many social routines grew out of making of tools on the shores of lakes?

Design is a communication across time as much as it is about communities and personal relationships, as they were then or as they presently exist. On top of this is the utility served by the craftsman, and on top of this is the human cure for boredom. Art has these in common as well.

In order to make things easier, in order to survive and maybe to thrive, vision from the very stones lying on the earth became actual things. The axe which came to exist, out of our mind, out of seeing possibilities. These are stone tools, but a form of technology nonetheless, this is precision. In a place where the one doing the designing was considering both problem and solution simultaneously there came cerebral progress, loads of it. This may not have been about the individual item being developed, more so of what might be accomplished with contemplation in all its variations, it is not so much an instrument as it was a choice.

Need - Job - Industry

When it was combined with craft it became an automatic relationship of hands-on work.

When with that of performing one task (making a tool) being before doing another task (hunting or cracking nuts), this was bred with qualitative decision making. Sometime before this the order was reversed, but when the tools were proven to work they became the priority. We will go hunt after the axes are ready.

It gives us the evidence that stages were considered in what work needed to be performed. Planning was involved as much as technique and the memories of just how to execute the steps. Sounds like design, sounds like best practices.

On many similar lake shores where many similar seeds were sewn, is a growth point of all the mental work that went along with newly adopted technologies. A series of inter-personal techniques were being welded to the use of tools, the physical work became associate with having a plan, things were getting cerebral.

If this means that we have witnessed our first sort of craftsman then did in fact we see the adoption of a new way of living. One where everyone mobilized and organized? This may be a leap, but what we do know is this is the first human home of specialization. If a few individuals were best at making hand tools then from that would they find the desire to trade tools for other items? Is this possible?

Is there a consideration of production, if there was a designated location of an individual who simply made axes all day then they would have generally mastered the methods upon which trade was based?

All of this dating back to 100,000+ years ago, it is extremely hard to say, but the lines are basically drawn where all was eventual. When the first 'specialized' axes were hammered out from bone onto stone we had truly evolved insight.

> *"man is a tool-using animal...without tools he is nothing, with tools he is all."*
>
> Thomas Carlyle (1795-1881)

The Axes of Time

There is a place in Southern Africa, known as the Klasies River Mouth. It was in this spot that a lifestyle of cave occupation went on circa 150,000 years ago, an obvious archeological hot spot.
Not all that far from it exists another couple of places, Kalambo Falls & Olorgesailie, these in the East of Africa. Specifically here the same lifestyle was ongoing circa 200,000 years ago.

This was of successive human occupations, some series of setting up of the usual manner of hunter & gatherer groups and moving around a bit. The later site was discovered in 1953 by Desmond Clark. This location revealed a cache of Acheulean style hand axes. One actual finding was within the dark clay and white sand around the falls. The special shapes were attributed to being formed from wooden clubs, indicating tools for making other tools.

> *"These axes, made of local materials, were shaped by human hands. Here, fire was also present. In this location alone over 400 axes were found, in what perhaps could be seen as an ideal location."*

Desmond Clark

It was indeed a staging ground, built to produce axes and many of them. This is possibly the oldest find of tool on tool technique, where bone was used to fine tune blades by 'micro-flecking'. Here would have been a mind bend for the club carrying cave man. It was near or somewhere in the region that new levels of details were given to both how tools were produced and how they were made in abundance. This place was a game changer.

Out of this place these individuals hunted what included a minimum of 65 types of animal species. Including a style of hunting which encircled types of baboons in the trees along the river. Those that lived in this advanced style camp were elite hunters, studying tactics as well as arsenals. For this there was a need for the teachings of specialized tools (study of Olorgesailie).

Along it came, the fine tuning, the evolution of the handaxe, as if through observation & insight, as to how these items performed in the field. Designed, built and tested all along the same river banks. Tied together with it came the techniques of further refinement. This may have been difficult, but hugely rewarding.

- From simple pebble tools to the removal of the sides & surface.
- Elongated, teardrop shape characterized the style
- Pointed end & broad end
- The basic round blade shape improved over time
- The ability to make tiny changes as 'flecks' were removed.
- Creating larger straighter edges, for the purpose of cutting.
- Pointed at one end, rounded at the other, retouched, refined.

This was all the work of Homo Sapiens, those dwelling in these productive locations, they who set up shop and had left ample evidence of their work in piles around their caves along the rivers.

An all-purpose piece of cutting equipment was one of the results of unknown years of retooling. With it they had a technology capable of cutting, sawing, digging, bashing, preparing food, and boring holes. That is a highly developed result from anyone's perspective, and it all sounds an awful lot like design.

"the form is a shape inside a piece of stone and in the mind of the maker."

Desmond Clark

This particular variety of hand-axe became a more complex tool than it appears, it is from a process just as complex. From its creators, fully aware of what they needed as an end product, this most definitely is a product by anyone's standards.

To develop this involves a complete modification of a stone cobble. It eventually emerges as a highly refined instrument in the end. It possesses a symmetrical outline. This in itself reflects its purpose, one that when applied will require further skill to use it. The craftsmanship requires skill and foresight as well as an ability to manufacture a consistent item, over and over again.

Individual materials were selected according to known criteria, the cobbles had to be 10 – 15 cm to create a smaller axe, and up to 30 cm long for the larger axes. The oldest axes, those of the Acheulean style, came from the Konso-Gardula region of South Ethiopia. These were dated at 1.9 million years ago and were likely produced by early Homo Erectus rather than Homo Sapiens. There also exists a site of discovery dating back 700,000 years old in Kenya, known as the Kilombre where similar work was performed.

"Many of these tools were similar in size, providing

the notion of 'idea' behind the design and the crafting of an axe. If they were descriptively similar then there is a form necessary to 'be' the end tool."

Desmond Clark

This carrying out of craft as well as technique has been somewhat consistent for a very, very long period of time given what has been unearthed. The individuals whom have etched it out this way so long ago have not only based it on necessary qualities of a tool but one of the vision to make a classic shape, style & design. This is the root bearing the context as well as paradigm from which the 'crafter' comes from, a culture, a social continuum.

The activity of thinking is also one of 'reduction', and for this an intelligence is required. Add to this the technique and the development of a consistent process, in order to maintain the outcome as well as the quality, this being the proper length of the axe. To form this item time and time again with the same length to width ratio indicates a 'plan' and a certain mental aptitude. Here would be the imagery from the crafter's, and in the case of Kilombe, true craftsmanship.

*The Acheulean name is based upon artifacts from the Northern France area of St. Acheul.

In Europe there have discoveries of like objects, but with a much cruder design. Generally speaking these have irregular edges lacking the symmetry and refinement as well as were chiseled with heavier flakes. Not all things were equal. The find in Western Europe came from meltwater created by a melt period between glaciations. Typical river terraces & river valleys in the 19th century were the sites of discovery, such as near Abbeville & St. Acheul.

Over time the designs of the axes, although slowly, became straighter and more aligned edges were characteristic. It is known that at least 2 techniques were common over this time period. The stone-on-stone method is considered the 'hammer technique' that provided the earlier irregular shapes (D. Clark). The other is the bone/antler method, referred to as the 'soft technique' and it resulted in the smooth regular forms of axe. This was the more sophisticated and easier to control method where the desired amount of removal was given. The thinner and wider flakes became the newer process and the attention to detail evolved more rapidly.

In such locations as St. Acheul, cleavers were found. These were characterized by broader blades and more leading edges. Also discovered were scrapers, borers & burins, which were used for engraving.

Another design style was the Clactonian, from locations in England. Like the Acheulean types had models that were made more quickly and rudimentarily for the purpose of specific tasks, this being the specific activities they were needed for, the crude type. In its own right this is also a design paradigm, the rapid product for a basic requirement, nothing fancy, just lots of them. Once again, characteristic of Fordism style in general. These were formed using whatever materials were on hand, perhaps even opening the question – to make an axe did one need to use good material?

There exists also the Oldowan series of artifacts. These were simple tools, made from pebbles. Most were choppers, notches & denticulates, and there were no axes.

Time Periods

Homoerectus, as they are known, have been around for 2 million years, this after the beginning of the Pleistocane period. From here came the technologies, the hand-axes, the more basic tools, the fire control. Humans specifically were exclusive to Africa and in Africa for 3 million years before they moved onto the North.

The move revealed new problems, which required new and innovative solutions. In that list certain skills included cooking for foods, making of clothes, development of family structure and eventually the making of society. Yes, as it turns out society was an eventual development, and a cultural membrane at that.

Modern Humans came about during the end of the Pleistocene period, this encompassing the time of 200,000 to 130,000 years ago. Here it is thought to have come under the developments of nurturing and ritual. Fully modern humans, those of Homo sapiens sapiens, are evident from the Upper Paleolithic era, those discussed with the Klasis Caves of 100,000 years ago. Biologically indistinguishable from ourselves, they branded art, advanced tools and tailored clothes. Homo sapiens-

Neanderthal Lensis, of about 200,000 years ago, were replaced by modern humans somewhere around 50,000 years ago, this to the best of our knowledge.

Designing Above Time

More, is always better, when growing products is concerned. When these can be malleable, changed around according to fit, it shows that the developmental pattern is evolving for the user & designer as well. When something 'not yet existing' is modified solely in the mind there is a designer's whim to make it as useful as possible. This even though something can be useful even when it does not exist. This can even take the form of tools, clothes, ideas or techniques.

What about when the occasion arrives when items need to be very hard, very enduring, out-endure the craftsman themselves. This is another level of planning, that with Deep Design intentions.

This is when something can be made to last and last, generations. For an item to fit so well into a use that it almost seems automatic. There are five categories needed for something to fit this, these describe the hand-axes.

- Something that returns to the same spot/state.
- Something that doesn't change.
- Something that physically can remain in the same state for many decades.
- Something that is rudimentary enough that it cannot

evolve beyond a certain development, it cannot be improved.

- Something that possesses intrinsic meaning or value right from its beginning.

In a situation where the community was using all the axes that one craftsman could possibly make, or within the populace where not requiring all the tools the group of craftsman were making provides a broad stretch as per a community and for commerce. This being that there would possibly be trade for those finished items, but even if each member made their own axes, there would be a need for a school of sorts, where techniques would be taught. This is obvious due to the consistencies in the evolution of the tools themselves, this would further organize productivity.

This would have been the concept of being organized, having patterns and creating efficiency. These are big big steps, as is merely associating cavemen with production of quality end use products for the masses.

Mass Production

Strategic although specific materials were at the center of the process. Those became selected as part of the visual aspect even before action of experimentation ever took place. What were the best materials? How difficult are they to find? And what were the best materials for shaping *those* materials? All questions considered in the infancy of the undertaking. These answers all would have a psychological bearing on the makers of tools. On the wandering tribes who looked for resources across the lands. Due to its makeup, an axe would have a significant impact on each the user, the target and on society. This is the nest of technology in general and its implications overall.

Next would come the messaging of the prototypes. Here is where the real work would begin, how just to tweak it to get more out of the initial design, to improve it to the point of perfection. This is where brains gained traction over brawn, and it made things really fascinating.

Perhaps, at these crossroads in ancient history we can draw some connections. At this intersection of being the maker with something that had yet to be made we see a solidification that enough had been learned that demonstrates that learning itself had become the primary practice. Our individuals were developing an edge over their environment. These were interesting times.

From this conclusion we can make a few attributions unto Deep Design itself. It houses a few characteristics within its curve of learning no matter when this takes place.

- Design is a process
- Design is not necessarily style
- Design is not just an end product but an advantage, as in using hand-made objects
- Design is as much about the method, as it is about the optimal tool, which is produced from that process

Encapsulation

Ending with what would be considered the design phase would no doubt come the final reactive effects. With this would come the larger picture, the one where littler details provide bigger implications. Once finality of a design happens, then the game turns to something else, such as waste and cost are considered, with what it takes to form many rocks and realize many axes there come economies of scale. Art shifts to production.

The first part relates to the importance of presence, 'the capturing of' a subject into an object, as in prototypes. This would give rise to a sense of 'value'. The second part is that of utility, the duplication of the original idea, to the gain of some societies or tribes.

In the beginning, as the instinct is toiling away at creating some object, to solve some obvious dilemma, things happen. Amongst the process as solutions are crafted out in the natural place of whim, is some form of intuition, an idea where something is heading. This is that, it is work, but effort in following some manner of knowing what is beyond mere chance.

Visualization has occurred, as some idea is borne into a physical sense. This is the difference between the seeking of vision and the seeking of craft, where work is concerned this is where the rubber meets the road.

It is as if, despite any value to end users in general, what happens is not generic and cannot be redundant in how it is done. Something useful requires the art step to happen first, that of instinct. The idea of things becoming more and more solid and into the tangible a process distills an outcome.

Here the artist must leave behind all that something *can*

be, and fine tune it into something it *is*. This is reliant of the scope of skill of the individual artist. The process itself is a bit more defined, as like transfer out of the virtual into the objective. Art meets production.

What we do know is many axes were made, as in specific places and in all likelihood by more than one person. It seems to resemble mass outcome.

"the mind penetrates"

Neil Challenger & Jacqueline Bowring

Chapter Two–
The Path of the Projection Process

"seeing it a certain way outside the usual line of sight"

Mathew Collings

As someone is busy working out the makeup of some inspiration, some idea, or is simply following through as seeing where some item is developing, there exists a certain distillation process. A tendency of this the search is perhaps an analysis for the end result. With this pathway to the end result there is much mystery and much unknown, this is all part of the designing process. The ability of the developer or artist to focus on the activity within certain parts the action and other parts thought, there also exists instinct and guesswork. It is a fascinating endeavor. Just in bringing out how it all unfolds & happens, is a major point. Here we should include an aspect of raw witnessing by the craftsman of their own work as it would be for any bystander. If the unique pathway to the end result was known then there would be very little bother with special artistry in general.

Mind & Human

It had been the Greek civilization, which we first know of, to offer status to honor something. They generated ideas about flow, power, realism, inspiration & of course alternate perceptions. It presented possibilities, alternate

28

ways of considering reality.

Art, in the modern sense, performs a breakdown of this. It distils and breaks apart established ideas all at once, both showing them for what they are as well as revealing other directions. In this case there must exist baffling possibilities, and this *is* the point, where draining established values and status from objects is the idea. We see this with post-modernist movement of art works, and hence in the social matrices of thought, which becomes art, a license perhaps, to mash things up a bit, and to show their faults or pretenses.

What remains is the practice of art itself, and perhaps as it relates to philosophy in a broad picture sense. The creative sort of item, which brings about the optimism in the first place, becomes the cultural icon. That manner of bringing these pillars to the surface is both the role of the designer and the artist, bringing about change and with that comes result, and upon this design creates cultural shift.

"art: the possibility of deafening chaos"

Mathew Collings

Developing patterns, this becomes the means of fixing or of altering an image. Great design schools of thought, such as minimalism have with it a near religious following, a nearly cult like adherence to the methods of creativity & functionality. This is the nest of development for the big picture stuff, where flow and change must continue intermixed, to be what a design must display to those who witness it. Typically in religious circumstances there is some recognition of an order greater than us, something that goes out there and relates to a spirituality within each of us. It usually contains the singular purpose of heading off the chaos in an effort to extinguish it. Here we see a difference between art & design at their cores.

In a studied state where students work on ideas, relationships exist amongst physical things, a process itself. Within it is our physical manifestation of the modern abstract form, those simple or complex products built by designers to create a marriage of form & function while considering how to make many copies for many individuals. Our current attempt at making it all make sense is also our attempt at pulling our thinking away from any sheer randomness, but this is actually hard to do and ever more difficult to describe. It is due to the underlying fact that designing minds experience acts & flights of randomness while annealing towards solutions. Randomness is part of the process, and without it who knows if people are doing the finding, people are random.

Design conceptualization, tends towards completion, slowly cornering our ideas out of a method borne of transferal of another collage of preexisting knowns. This is how the human mind distills the process, one where we can work things out and just see what is in there. A lot of this is based on patterns, classical uses for designs, and meshing with the unknown changes we wish to apply to things. Updates if you will from these established constants are more of modification than originality, but can stir our perceptions and only a few minor changes can revolutionize our culture.

Within the development of a tool, how it looks, how it fits in the hand, how it feels, are the simplicities which make them iconic. A hammer will always look rather like a hammer, even with a little variance in geometry, because this is the conclusion of a need as it meets the human hand.

When do tools become beautiful, when is the symmetry just right for it to be none other than such? Do these highly refined objects find their way into our normal ways of life? Is this the point where we are satisfied with the lasting endurance of what we have created. This is the opposite of chaos, it is the human control of materials.

The Design Box Model

A problem becomes, when it becomes defined, existing by its overall outline, and here the part of it that is the internal problem has to then be fully defined.

Below is an illustration to try and relate a conceptual understanding of how it is to bring an idea along its timeline to full maturity. This represents a model where an idea begins in the back, and progresses towards the front.

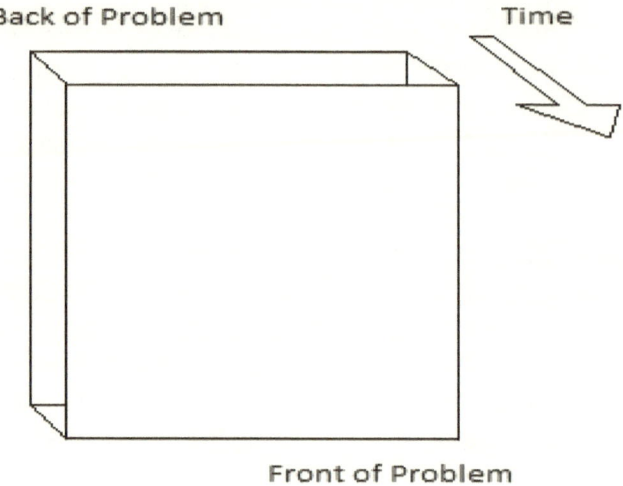

Back of Problem   Time

Front of Problem

Fig 1: Creativity Box

In the back, are the details of a problem, the first face or the beginning of the design. The front on the other hand is the destination, and remains largely hidden from the designer until the problems have been sorted out. Perhaps it is fair to say that it is an A to B journey, two faces with many problems in the middle which require solving. As one works their way to the front things become more clear and mature and the end result becomes more visible. This comes only after distinct choices have been made. The front is largely based on the time investment needed to get there, it is what the public sees.

The back is much like an initial napkin sketch, heading towards the front is basically a flow by which developments happen towards a final product. This is based on solving all of the arising problems within the box itself in the life of an evolving item and the techniques needed to make it.

The first step of the journey comes in the immediate space away from the back face. As this is the starting position it is where everything begins. It is the face that is visible only to the designer. Getting through the box of problems involves mental time, as it contains the problems and the answers for a successful design. Spanning the distance between the 2 takes many steps and is the actual work that goes into making a successful product. Getting across the distance of the box may be a fast leap or it may take centuries or generations to get everything just right.

The Front

As an audience this is what I would see, the final product, the end result. This is the face of the idea that sees daylight. All other things, being the contents of problems & solutions arrived at as well as the back face are hidden from me. All that matters is that I see the arrival point as a usable functional item. At any time in history the front face would be the determined end point of product design.

Having endured the idea and the trials & tribulations of progress from sketch-to-delivery the inventor has given every effort to get it here. This is what we witness as consumers, the end product, the end result, all that is simple and user friendly.

There are many people in the population that never think beyond the generalizations of an object, this is a car, that is a kettle. It is the developer's job to be the opposite of this so that many can enjoy the luxury of loose acceptance. It is quite okay, after all it is the role of each face of the design box model. This defines the roles played out in society, a separation. Many things are invisible on purpose and just what it takes to get solutions to be hidden is a great deal of effort and success.

The Back

Towards any decent idea comes the place and point where the effort begins, the initiation of some cerebral translation of that idea. This is where designers begin their journey into the physical. It is often a baby step in an invisible direction in the hopes of finding a very visible solution.

It is the natural place for innovation, the beginning of invention and expression, where we realize people have made full use of their creations. The beginning of a fabric of thought, between the theoretical & the tangible, a space between the *could be* & the *is*. Becoming the literal ground where artist generates craft into solutions. By this view we see the view of the inventors. This is no easy path to strike out on, as someone somewhere at some time has to start into some unknown, and into doing it for the first time.

There is actual documentation that crows are smart enough to understand how water displacement works, by dropping rocks in small containers of water they can lift things to the surface. This too is where the monkey is at, they have thought out the way to use crude tools to access food to eat. This is quite smart, and each behavior shows promise and a clever aptitude within situations. It is

34

the human that shows the capacity to step into an innovative role and completely remake what already exists in the physical word. This is where people found their footing in nature, to see and to express.

How was it that the cave dwellers thought to take one stone, perhaps a specific type of stone, and use it to manipulate the shape of a second stone. This was to bear fruit rather quickly, but what was the lightning bolt that began the process to use specialization? It is the question of how this interlaces with not need, because honestly they were surviving with or without it, but luxury. Having many tools available, tools whose uses were wide and varied, this is where it came down to the perception of options, to see them and to play them out. It is the item that makes imaginations into people, and cave men into craftsmen. The pressing out of mentally shaped images unto the world, as if out of thin air they developed were what we call the prototypes.

Having gone to great effort to press the mental image into the rock the person altered something, something worth knowing. Whereas before it was not certain it could be done *now* it was just known that it was doable, manipulation had occurred. This is a watershed moment in events, this is the first step into the great unattainable. Existence was never the same after that moment had been fulfilled. Do we know how many planetary years back it happened, no, but this much we realize did happen for certain.

It would be safe to count that at this point there was a massive period of experimentation. Many screw-ups and blind successes followed in getting those first stones into being those first axes, but you have to admit it was some level of brilliance.

So here sat Bub the stone carver and likely some of his friends for countless hours, those who had some free time, working away perhaps on what we may dub a spinoff innovation, and with the focus of a task that had never been done before, that of crafting. And with these days and weeks and years of chipping away we have a process of learning to manipulate the items, both the directing stone & the tools of stone, for greater and more specific outcome. In design this would sound an awful like technique, those required for any industrial design.

As Bub and company held the power to manipulate large quantities of stones they began the long slow unfolding of learning and skill. A lot of this would have been how to select each stone, how to hold the bashing stone, how to use pinpoint force to direct energy into the tool stone, and other specialities like how to get a certain depth out of a series of strikes. Because we were not there to witness the massive leap forward we are left to picture what it may have been like. Within the pathway of Bub's learning there must have been a second step. Much like the first blind step where a visual seed of changing the form of a stone into something more specific we would have to think that here again there was further expertise. Now that Bub had digested what he or she had accomplished it was time to imagine a more specific shape, one that could very well 'look' a certain way. This is the application that design is compressed into and manifested out of. With this envelope of taking what had been gathered up mentally Bub would be able to transfer knowledge into what at first could not be seen, all of this because Bub spurred himself to get off his log on some sunny day.

Once the new image had manifested itself, and combined with what had become known, we would now have witnessed the dawn of craftsmanship & focus to detail. It is certainly due to the fact that Bub had made an impression on him or herself and now wanted to proactively steer everything into a focused direction thereafter. The stone as striking tool and product tool had arrived and so with it had the future.

Bring in the antler as striking object, this is a beyond guessable technique, this was the high watermark for the time, for advanced & specific blades could be formed repeatedly. Bub came into a totally different thing altogether, a paradigm shift of unknowable potential, this was the birth of high quality products.

At some unknown time, enough method, know-how and experimentation had taken place where by the object used for making a product had changed, from a stone to an antler. With it came higher control of the delivery of force and the absolute outcome of the flecking of stone chips out of rocks. It was magnificent, it was exact. As antler proved so far superior a forming tool and by which exact amounts and sizes of flecks could be shed that once again an evolution had occurred in tool design. It was allowing symmetrical edging, specific canting, optimal weight, balance, pointed tips, elongation, narrowing and customization for objects. Add to that was an easy replication using this method. It must have been simply amazing.

The Sum of Parts

It may well have been a sunny day a few generations later, either the offspring of Bub or a far distant relative who managed to get all of the stubborn questions sorted out. In some way there could have been a few gaps in the technical know-how, but looking for chronology in this road-map is pointless.

The steps took place, this we know absolutely. Within using the antler and within knowing technique and outcome gave the Bub family a gain in sense of what was going on within the materials themselves. These highly defined and massively produced tools were making a difference in their lives and certainly who they were as individuals. It was allowing the accretion of food in different ways, evolution of hunting, it was facilitating preparation of food with hand tools, it was resulted in chopping, cutting and shaping of soft materials like wood, it was a man-made effect onto the world. World meets design.

It was here that we see the steps beginning to culminate. It was the beginning of something big, and it was unstoppable at this point because there was without a solitary doubt, a psychological impact upon those living in and around Bub's community. Others had witnessed it, even if they could not comprehend it, they would had come to know change. Perhaps there were even moments where these humanoids actually saw no boundaries to just what the axe & other tools could accomplish. There existed another step, that of shaping pieces that work together, parts all working to congeal as a whole end result, the shaping of lifestyles.

Tools were undoubtedly necessary for building homes, using long fabric strands, making fences, then agriculture. Whenever this happened for the first time tools were undoubtedly present, and were needed to craft future instruments like the bow & arrow or even a boat. Tools were most likely there the first time a fishing net was made, and the methodology for just how to use them. Not forgetting that an axe need a handle but perhaps the greater union of many parts was still a distance down the road, conceptually the perfect axe or tomahawk was inevitable.

Chapter Three–
Design & Paradigm

'Design is communication.....even across time.'

Johnathon Glancy

A par-a-digm is more than a word, it is actually a number of things and each of these to differing types of people. Technically meaning model or something in association thereof, it is something of a floating word, existing somewhere between a noun and a sort of verb. It is in one sense a thing about some set of actions, but having rules. On another sense it is an objective item. This is a scientific outline, as well as having sociological indications. Such items can contain separate intonations, possibly those belonging to...designers. Is this that much different from an archetype or a pattern? The word also has linguistic character. It can infer choices within linguistics as well as exclusion. Has it made things somehow simpler to understand? That depends, on whether you see the use as an action or an object. In another sense it is a word about a manner of how to organize or separate thoughts. For each discipline there exist individual paradigms all relating to different conclusions.

Epistemology, as we know it, is a theory or theories about knowledge itself. It is a kind of sub-frame to what it means to know things. There are commonalities to the variances of what can be known, there can be examples such as models, for instance the delivery of attaining parts of knowledge about some process. It fits a pattern, one that is repeating, which is easy enough to identify as such. Here is where it goes leading into some raw paradigm. It is that while something a person carries out is performed, and by this there are practiced set of techniques. With this are identifiable patterns of thought behind it.

Technical approach labels evidence as part of the method, and there must be a way to prove and disprove a possibility. If this were from a designer then there would be a school of reference, even a school of training. This is an archetype to mold where the development of thought has something to remain true to, for the most part. The undertone is the mindset, and that is really the point, that under disciplinary patterns there is to some extent a track to follow to get to one's destination and one's style. There is more than one track of possibilities depending on whom one is following.

The idea is that the bias follows more like the verb, in making something into a certain solution by a process in which parts are altered. Perhaps it's plastic into water bottles, or tubing into chairs. While each discipline is aware of many alternatives, they themselves remain unwavering. Thomas Kuhn coined this 'opaque', or the hidden back side beyond the box so to speak, beyond what can be seen from the beginning.

Generally speaking both chemistry & physics have a relationship with the encapsulation of paradigm, it has a specific principle. It has much to do with entropy and the changing of parts before the completion of reactions. Sociologists see paradigm as something of a 'worldview' held by groups of people. These have to fit in with a history of a group or within a shelf of ideas, many already preconceived, that are theoretically open to change. The tones of each are not all that different. Each acts as more of a guide being of the noun sort, as something turns through the pages of time.

They reside over products or solutions or creations as they course their way through the design stages.
Insight

If you were to dig around a bit, to pry somewhat at the way the last few thousand years has unfolded you would tend to pick something out. Growth and innovation leaps with fits and starts. After this it equally stops. They just seem to work this way, or rather behave in this manner. It is quite peculiar perhaps, and the more you look into things the more one begins to realize it has always been this way, design it seems is a roller-coaster ride and always has been.

It may just be events and causation, quite literally the case when earth shattering changes are ushered in. Likely under social progress, or otherwise under natural pressure maybe even societal upheaval. All those little innovative steps or jumps arrive on some occasion. Technologies are often like that. This all seems isolated, but gaining something predictable shows more patterns of near randomness. It is difficult to know just how it all operates and how inventions appear. It is when the upheaval starts that ears perk up as alternatives tend to get more of our attention.

The activity of paradigm is smashing and is very noteworthy. All of a sudden out of nowhere things change. And directions are reformed. During a series of creative events, the shaking of lifestyles get some start and ignition of remaking what had gained acceptance. Where as in manipulating the way that things often fit together into a smooth curving run, all sounds very nice, it does not seem to work this way. Sometimes out from beyond the horizon things seem to shift, to come apart and then fit again together with new rules, this is alike the innovations and effects of art.

This is where there is no going back. When both the personal computer and the typewriter went head-to-head, it kind of turned the normality of daily life on its head, and we never saw things the same again. It is arguable whether or not this type of action takes place in the field of philosophy or architecture, we do hypothesize that it is one of the main pillars of design & of society.

If this is within the making of products then we could show the great example of German perfectionism vs. Russian Fordism, that seen in as the 1930's and gave way to the world of the 1940's. Here the earth laid witness to sheer industrial repetition conquering over refined engineering, to gain total dominant prowess. An event like no other took place and there wasn't much denying where we all ended up following this. Industrial Fordism was the new production of nearly all design.

Is this the cumulative tide of changing our ideas and attitudes of our fate, and the outcome as if sealed within mass production of everything from chairs to cars. When Fordism laid waste to perfectionism we experienced a generational shift of staggering proportions. Presently we may witness a sense that there is a new separation going on between design, thinking and the overall approach to making something fantastic. As often is initially fuzzy, the final outcomes are titled with 'how we got here' and 'where & why do we go next' ? Design overall seems to make more sense the farther you step back.

Anti-entropic style, the desire to change things up every now and again, is exactly what good design is about. Even architecture, as an overall paradigm gets bogged down from time to time. It is the restraint that comes with mannerisms. Otherwise referred to as a school of thinking it courses its way around the world and provides boundaries.

And so it begins, effort, the act of working within what is known as well as taught. As someone sits down at the drawing board and puts pencil to paper to accomplish something it first has to exist in the mind.

Hindrance & the problems are something else altogether. It's more a question of the establishment's capacity to grind out details, as within lay the answers. Here come the solutions & the alterations. It is much more like the microscopic change, whether still on paper or actually within the shop, this is under design, the making thereof something useful.

Getting on with it and producing the mental image of something like a bow & arrow can provide a rather immediate answer, based on just the basics of how difficult is it going to get. Rather it may become more intricate, arrows or something that then should fly. That is what makes actual things into wonderful & smart things, harnessing the aspects unmistakable, and probably the most definite part of the 'why not' mentality.

Thinking outside the box of rules is just what designers do. They set out with this intention and on a path to break things up a little. This is why art and design are less noun paradigms and much more acts of placing tangibility.

As goes etymology, it is still one step further back from getting one's hands dirty. Basically this is study done from within a desk view, where ambiguity is acceptable. As with the theory of knowledge it is not actually the same as the transformation that Bub himself went under. This was where on a particular day he considered something, and with it he stepped out there into a world of knowing it. This is a difference worth noting. It exists through hard work and within the reality that resides under great theories, the golden slivers of hard lessons. All the sweat and the blisters that were put into stone tools are of being absolutely certain of things when you came out the other side, because you played out the cards of your ideas.
Practice Makes Perfect

It seems that trial & error is central to knowing. To do so - is to know. If making the perfect boomerang, cutting it from the perfect tree, then getting out there on the grass and testing how it feels, how heavy the thing sits in the fingers, how it floats in the air, how it sounds as it is cupped by hands & held by the wind. Here the outside is the lab. Seeing what makes an object not predictable, this is the user experience of prototypes.

Design by far is more of a handling science, with industrial products, those readily available, things get hammered into being. Allowing skipping some of the creative steps, by using already prepared items, well even Bub would consider this central.

There is born a relationship, between experimentation and artist. One that will usually consume a great deal of time, one aimed at rewards. It is actually a type of mindset in itself, one where great 2 way communications happen, one where battles are won or lost. It is great fun, the many trials of any product.

Chance & Reason

For the same reason that both perfect order & perfect disorder are impossible and cannot actually be, there is also the same reason that by which both of these things are fundamentally the same thing. Everything is somewhere in the middle, and everything that is, is a propagating result of other things effecting it. This is complex pattern, and a pattern of chaos. It is the land of play amongst actual things.

The true utterance of type of movement is rather unpredictable, it is complex and hard to see. Almost as if 'you cannot get there from here' but you may get there all the same. It is the nonlinear activity of heaps and heaps of things all mixed in together. With one another the unforeseen, of the exciting, the dull and the lazy with the rapid all fluctuating.

Reason it seems has become incorporated with what it doesn't and simply cannot know, into a blindingly simple view, which has fair odds of working itself out in known ways. The chances are the mail will arrive at 10'o'clock tomorrow morning, but maybe, just maybe both the bag of mail and the man & the van delivering it were hit by lightning, just before your stop. If and when your packages fail to eviscerate into ashes by the handful via super-heated ions, then we have a probability your mail has survived. So what are the chances? Due to cavemen never waited around for their axes to be delivered by the post, which would have proved a gross waste of time, they better spent their time bashing away at things and running after and from things.

We do not have such lifestyles now as we practice our ideas, moving between product and intention. We usually have shops and laboratories and clean surfaces to work with. The difference is opportunity, and opportunity depends of course & obviously on the context.

When is it healthy to think outside of the realm of one's own boundaries, of one's own discipline? To propel one's self out of the box and come down with creative solutions is actual genius. How do you explain the specific difference between this and the caveman? Brilliant products are extremely difficult to make and rather often nearly impossible to predict. It is without a doubt that this is part of the product and design life cycle. Products that should have been scratched away at and rapidly made it to success rather often fail once they see daylight. Each condition is part of the process and knowing them all is difficult.

What makes it out into the public eye is and not separate from, complex order. As these items are not separate from reason they too should have some type of product lifespan. It is just that it does not have much to do with logic at any specific time. It has to do with people and populations, because chaos and reason are entwined. What are the odds that people would dig up and discover the relics and tools of nomads hundreds of thousands of years into a future? Probably pretty much no chance at all and yet it has happened. As well this may all happen again.

Chapter Four–
Tattoos in the Mind

As far as we can tell, there is little means to question that tattoos have been around longer than 7000 years. This provides us with a simple implication, that they are likely part of the human persona for at least this long. Here no one is saying nor providing suggestion that they cannot or will not date back any further. It is just that we are unsure about how far. Given these 7 millennia, as the coming and going of generations, there seems to have existed a craft, one with paint or ink onto skin.

From the Neolithic era there is as much evidence as to bolster this, but upon clay pots. It is perhaps from here too that no actual tattooed skin will ever surface for us to see, and this makes sense since it was a long time ago. It is rather more interesting the style of such carvings on these clay pots, those in repeating patterns as with many known tribal tattoos. If we can see that the designs etched into the pots themselves then is it such a foolish leap from clay to skin? Never the less these individuals were drawing, and while they were at it, if it meant so much to them, then why would they have stopped short of even charcoal & skin?

Otzi & the Princess

What we do know is that some well positioned hikers stumbled across the next best thing in the last days of summer during 1991, somewhere in the Otztal Alps. It was here, way up in the mountains where Austria & Italy meet, that something miraculous finally happened. People stumbled onto the iceman himself. Suspected to have been a shepherd 'Otzi' had lay in wait under the ice for 5000 years, and he was about to change the perceptions of some far-flung generations. The thing is he was covered in tattoos, 57 of them to be exact, all upon various spots, ankles, wrists, lower back, achilles tendon, and there was more. His clothing was all well intact, his weapons and tools were present and accounted for and Otzi it would appear had a lot to say about himself. As a European of the copper age, he came delivered into the future with all of his skin well preserved, bearing crosses, lines and small marks, and in markedly fine shape. It was clear the tattoos had been placed upon him with charcoal into incision by someone else, as if for some good reason. It is just that he wasn't able to tell us just what those intentions were specifically, but they were there all the same. Also provided with Otzi came the realization that acupuncture was in fact both practical and used in his area and during his time & lifetime. Something we now know and are no longer surprised by.

Across a great vast distance, to his east, out there in the Siberian republic of Altai, not long ago a girl was found in the summertime. She was discovered in a Kurgan, a type of burial mound, along with 3 horses and had been there, frozen for 2400 years. She had with her the tattoos she had received within her 25 years of life, almost perfectly preserved across this long expanse of time since. Such elegance of the work on her epidermis was considered part of the Pazyrks style. Here it is thought that the goal was to make, as one grew older, one's body as beautiful as possible. It was in this culture within eastern Russia, that several mommies became marked with skin art. Along with the young lady were her two warriors, a norm associated with an Ukok princess. They also possessed very intact and elegant representations on their skin. Turns out these were held by nobles & nomads alike. Mythical and realistic they were made in various poses, and usually of the animal or celestial varieties.

Parallels Across Time

Grounded in the natural world, and its possible fit with some astrological themes, maybe amongst a variety of tribal arts tattoos don't seem so out of place in modern times. It seems there weren't many ways to receive a tattoo. The majority are charcoal and soot and placed using a skin penetrating instrument by a small incisions, rather like they are today.

How many examples of ancient body ink can we look at? Was this all going on independently? Yet these tattoos all have many things in common. This is from the representation as well as belief. The methods and the nature of the tattoos themselves are symbols of designs placed upon the body. What then was the bigger idea?

Some indications are that status was assigned to each tattoo, some for being a warrior, others for being chief. In the Maori, what is called Ta Moko, where the whole face & body ensemble is marked, which are both difficult as well as painful, they contain elements for right-of-passage. In some of the more abstract art the owner were those who were Shaman. Mommies all over the archaeological scope have held tattoos, on wrists, arms, torsos. Some tribal sects such as the Picts, had many rather lovely body markings, and preferred to keep them under their clothing. But none of this can be proven for the way things were with previously frozen Otzi.

In other cases skin art was forced upon the losers of battle, such as the Sumarians & the Romans. They actually did this to each other at different times. Out of a visit to Tahiti came the actual word, or so it is thought, by none other than Captain Cook. He misspoke the local word 'tatau' as tattoo. That is how things went. The number of civilizations having worn tattoos is long. It encases the North with the Celts, the East with the Egyptians, the South with Polynesians and the West with Aboriginal culture. Tattoos it seems have made their way around the entire world and for various reasons. It has been as such for quite some length of time. There are actually many kinds of artwork, but the patterns are repeating, images of animals, fantastical hybrid creatures, languages of symbol, line, circle & abstraction, some are detailed & very handsomely complex.

Parallels Within Tattoo

Invariably it is considered the shoulder, especially over the left shoulder, and always has been for the common tattoo. There are also schools of patterns, such as the Eurasian style that both Otzi & the Siberian princess had belonged to. Here exist an archetypical approach, in the methods and the message. More often than not the discoveries of mommies included the finding of clay creations such as pots, where the body art had some common theme. No one can say for certain that these followed the same ideas as worn by individuals at the time the pots were detailed, but there is implication. By this there are a great many examples of just how involved these designs had become. It was a visual participation of the skin, to becoming part of the overall story of the person, their character and the path they took through their life. Here things are unmistakable. Also consider that at the time the manner of 'giving' a tattoo and the techniques applied would have qualified as technology, and perhaps they were adorned, as the individuals drawing them onto skin.

This, as much as artistic were much a spiritual way about schools of thought, that seem to become loaded into the very idea of a tribe. Common ways of looking at the world became described in the arts & crafts, objects as well as self.

Desire

What do tattoos say about their use, and about all of us? It is an uncertain guess, but it seems all the more likely that it may relate to some reference of mind. In this we may simply be relating a type of visual perception unto the body, obviously one that has become rather timeless. This is a constant, the same way a tattoo is permanent, that is the whole point. This exists aside from personalization, what it indicates to ourselves. But also what we belong to it clearly shows within its patterns, as Otzi and the princess each held a signal of just what they themselves were made of. They are a stylish and visual objective housing a rather dense subjectivity of the soul. Within this actually lies all that is the same and yet different for the working of the design category. Those where the unknown gradually gave into learned patterns and success. Once here it is easy to see the spectre of identity, as art has it. It is approaching the outcome and moving towards attaining self-knowledge, this is where the bridge exists.

The feeling of desire is strongly related to passion, a usual description within the disciplines of art & architecture. The scope itself that body & ink are ever-lasting can certainly have this too. A set of preferences they take in our lives, the shape of what we choose to think and work with in ink or in stones. It takes hold as a certain craft work, but there are feelings associated with putting them down into physical representation and then again as we view them, in some seat of permanence.

Chapter Five–
Architecture Versus Design

"Architecture has always been an instrument to willfully alter the world, or to spread the rumor that an architect has altered the world"

Keller Easterling

A to D

Many times over the years it comes to a question, that of the difference between architecture & design? How is it actually that 2 such creative outlets share common ground, and yet are not doing the same thing? Is it similar in our everyday thoughts or more so in the impressions given by how each is presented to us, each and every day, in the aesthetic purpose of each? Is it actually without doubt that we can hold one and not the other personally? Do the items developed by either belong to artist or to society in general? For it is a fungible item created from groups of attitudes, this value as to whether something is pretty or not, or whether seems useful or not. We as societies develop these modes of thinking and the perspectives by which we come to appreciate objective items.

It is true that designers and architects appreciate the inner & outer workings of objects in rather different ways. Designers sweat the small stuff so you don't have to, while architects picture the big stuff so that you may pause and delight in the small stuff. Given that we could escalate our thinking with either creative process it would seem that art itself is pretty at home with either school.

If physical manifestation is more your style then at the simplest point these 2 titans seem equivalent. Objectively strong but expressed differently, even if for the same person seeing them. Big bold lines are for buildings and the like, whereas the hidden workings and mysterious parts are more for the design enthusiast than architects. But at the same time each system has to work very well with anyone using them, each has to be people friendly and even fun to use.

Giving into an emotional attribute it could be alluded to that architecture speaks the loudest and considers the future of civilization ever more. This would be true except that tools and smaller items that we use in our hands every day, even without thinking about them, shape who we are and how we think and do things. This is highly influential.

What about us as people, what about us in our conquest within nature, in our struggle against what we are given to work with? Is it that empire or widget speaks more for our thousands of years of thinking and effort to preserve our existence? This is a good question, and on the first glance it would appear that structures like bridges and pyramids would be the answer. It is in the shadows of the human brain though that the real answer is provided. Inside of the compact and the small is the memory of how to use and equally the technique to quickly make and use something that is more our size. It is design that says much more about our species that any big picture stuff.

It is true that beautiful things are where we prefer our image, but designers must create and articulate details. They must transfer their composition of material into universally useful items that can be quickly made use of. It could be something for catching food, or something for fixing a dangerous problem. It is design that provides us our existence. It is an art all its own. Tools are our salvation. It is where people get their powers.

Speed and adaptation are 2 elements rarely associated with architecture. Churches take hundreds of years to construct from stone. It takes both systems working together to make populations happy about what they are, but the aspects of both are so very opposite.

Image

Compliance to the bigger picture, to keep a true eye on what is going on, the artist needs to not get bogged down with the method of communication. Having it close to them, to their heart is how designers & architects are artists, and not simply mechanical. These are the elements of inspiration that their crafts must work with, carrying their baby through to the end.

Materializing things, from mental sketches, those of the mental imagery, is a human's doing what they do best. This is the bare bones of an endeavor.

It becomes a careful game of teasing out what they first visualized, now into the physical. The way each handles their own paintbrush is true to their profession. Both architect & designer must deal with a fair amount of uncertainty along the way and concern themselves with different problems.

But here becomes a paradox. Here within the lines of the message and creativity comes a great span amongst the perspectives. This lives in the troublesome idea of time itself. Can something change over time, because design filters itself in an ongoing basis. If some physical manifestation *is* the architect than this will no doubt be torn down someday and rebuilt as something else. Are tools like this? Here is the point where the change in human style wins out over the craft. Giving into adaptation and throwing away prototype is a solid aspect of people. With this so is art, as humans change their minds or give up on the path of things they require objectivity that can follow their subjectivity. The more transferable the craft the more it may move along with them, and not become relic. We are constantly tearing things down and setting them back up.

Art, as an object purely of the mind, seems to override time. It is far less fallible as the years go by. Its mistakes, its oversights, are thought differently. Architecture is not quite like this. It itself is highly affected by time, the outcome of ongoing thinking and feeling. It is contemporary, it is fashionable, it is raveled in with people's attitudes when they observe it. This is because people are emotional about what they see.

Design is different than architecture. It includes only as many parts as are needed to do the job. If this is cutting of hair, then the scissors are rudimentary. If this is a place to sit then it needs only to resist gravity, if this is the hammering nails than the tool itself becomes basic and classic. But architecture is vulnerable to these extra simplicities. It fails the time game when it adopts the frills. It is often hard to resist, architecture becomes time awkward.

Art and design, as with the drawings made unto them, can exist without options, without extras. That is to say they serve the craft purely, and have the ability to keep classics up and running for a very long time. It is a near irony that when trying to not bring about attention on the tool, but to just how it works, that for it an irreplaceable object is born.

On the other hand, considering a capacity to remain vital and central, architecture remains this. It too can exist without the very options that compartmentalize it. This is an undertone, it is what separates design from architecture, although frills are sometimes fun they are separate. It seems rather small but instills a vast difference within itself and to all the people using things every day.

People

Capturing the trends of human life, and capturing the styles for living is a double edged sword. These fashions can come on heavily with influence and later boomerang into an eyesore. It's the ideologies which makes architecture 'heavy' and this perhaps means there is no way out. People will sooner or later change how they live. Strangely enough it is like art in its desire, in its emotional appeal and trajectory. In being and delivering some absolute job, the burden of being an architect is a tricky one.

People enjoy the strange, people enjoy variety. Over many years such different versions of idealism form a palette, one that develops taste. This selection gives way to a different type of cultural establishment, it gives rise to people reflecting and thinking about what they see and just what they think.

An architectural spectrum with many varied types of ideas, gives rise to a sort of method all of its own. It isn't that we need architects, it's that we like them. It is the same way we like selection, an option that eventually says something about us usually in hindsight, but ever so occasionally about our future.

Connections

Somewhere between the maker and the things made, the chairs, the flower pots, the bookshelves, we express ourselves. Architecture shows civilization, or perhaps what it could be, design shows what it is. Maybe this includes what mentality is just on the horizon as it is viewed as a whole.

The entire discipline seems to move slowly, whereas design moves at the blinding speed of the present, always a re-creatable and ever present making of things necessary.

Chapter Six–
The Personalization of Everything

Handbags, Bookshelves & Cats

Perhaps two of the easiest modern devises of all time may be the handbag & the shelf. It wouldn't take a great deal of imagination in accepting that both likely have existed for tens of thousands of years, minus perhaps the books that go into them. Bags are merely sacks, which may be made of any hide or plant material, and could be put together to make either convenience or necessity. Shelves are any horizontal flat material that can hold things.

Along way down the line, as things were mulled, crafted and perfected, came the room to make things much more specifically. To make them look & feel different from one another and to be special or unique to uses they had found. Here, in the moment of possible 'why' came an intention to make things easier and better. Here and eventually, the reasoning became that of 'because it suits me' and 'it's different than yours', all being part of such history of good devices.

A social revelation popped up, whereas previously any bags or shelves were simply just to hold things, to free someone's hands up so that they could get on with other things. This came after the gathering and mending, the designing of better items. Here came the personal bag. Obviously other than the plants and likely a few animal hides it took to assemble each bag, such would seem quite simple. But really the leap may have been carried out in the moment that individuality became part of the equation.

It is the question, how much of a difference was there before we each became involved, after all, we all get a kick out of bags and sacs that hold our stuff. If we did leave it alone, such as we simply assembled them and really had no insight into how we felt about each, then why make dyes?

This perhaps seems obvious, but non-the-less an innovation that became a social tool. It had in fact become a 'best of' craft as well as having a creative sense to it. In any manner it brings us along with the change, sweeping up societies and shaking down lifestyles. When the making of things improved came part of some other scene, one in which we could not see the implications. Now days companies go to battle over this kind of stuff, leading to all kinds of complexities. It is the behavior within us that promotes events of change and modification, the desire to customize. Things make their way out of the dark into being designed just for each of us and our perspectives. After all fancy products affect us. Then come new ways of thinking. Then life alters, and we are left with studying it all.

The true idea exists underneath it. As the taking of a rock, carving it, making it into something it was not previously, and then making all this mean something. This is more human than the simple object. This is personalization and it is how we make something more than it was in the beginning. How do we blow something up like this? Just like personalized pets for our humble homes, designer bred cats and other such things.

In the amount of time it requires to turn out an item, be it that of a shoe or a lamp, other items have already been discarded. Placed in a land fill or in a bin or on a mantle, people load the things they see with emotions. This may have something to do with expectation, or it may relate to past experience. Either way humans are an emotional bunch.

It is for this flavor of our reactions which make it feel like something new and when we use it we react to it. This brings to light something that is the *essence* of a product. Why does this mean anything to us? How can humans or any average individuals tie themselves in with what they are simply seeing or feeling, and together perceive reaction about a new thing?

This occurs even when an object is just sitting idle, perhaps just sitting there on the table. It seems built into the product with or without intent. It all comes from those carvings in the rocks as much as it comes from modern design schools, our reactions. Living with the items brings new modes of thinking and types of experiences that become not only realized, but adjustable thereafter. This is the world of stigma and loaded thoughts. Items come with use being bred into them, as imagery about the *state* of each object. Even when one is without the possession of the item itself the feelings persist. This is a reality particularly potent under the surface of perception.

Art functions along these lines, only indicating more or less what we do with mental imagery. In general art is without literal utility, it serves only what it means to. If this is devoid of application then art operates where other crafts simply cannot, without a pure physical purpose. When this is true then why, especially with the functional tone of design work, does all of it carry feeling?

On the one hand a person can argue that material objects are simply elevated by attitudes learned expectations & desires. Where merely the matter of letting the experience develop with perhaps something we have never seen before. On the other hand some people simply show no connection, they are simply disinterested or unaware. In some ways this is great design, where useful things go unnoticed just fitting into the background. Many professionals would see this as a high compliment, any artist would see this as insult, but it is an art all its own.

Whether items of distraction or items of special infatuation are common, much of this sort of thing is purposefully baked into the cake. Psychologically speaking we know enough to understand that learned response can be addictive for people. This comes from something known as design language, and now days it is the form by which objects speak to us visually.

This can work in a multitude of levels. If I see a bowl of buttons for the first time it certainly lacks the capacity to draw a mental imagery of 'what can I do with that'. But if I am introduced to my first spear, as for a caveman, this is different all together. Here I can realize its potential right away. Above this is some social consideration, the very way it could organize itself into groups of people. How can tools make groups adapt their behaviors? All the buttons in the world don't get us very excited, but give hundreds of villages spears and torches and cooking wood and you have yourself a social revolution.

This language also changes how we relate to products. It gives us a sense of who we are when we use them. Do we get a sense of slick modernism and elegance or do we feel bold and macho? Having all the cues all worked out in our heads is much of the transference of these subtle messages. They are unavoidable. Products are religious things, each born from separate methods of thinking that assist in defining who the users are.

The Vex of Oblivion

There is a mental place that has a home in an individual's hands. It does equally in the outcome of a society, a culture, a group or tribe. Only that each mental image has now been converted into physical form, into a man-made thing. Having the capacity to do that is rather powerful and it has gone down this way an unknown number of times throughout history. Blatantly knowing how something may 'tip' the scales is almost the same for a cave dweller as it is for a modern techno geek. This is the tender ground of individual perception, and it has an undertow for the things which we design, make and give. Unleashing creations onto the greater population has an obviously deep impact on its trajectory. Each mass of individuals takes form from its unpredictable things, and on down the road.

The idea of seeing open potential is one of the truly human aspects of our mind. It is more often than not indescribable to others outside of the initial vision, but not always. If ever there is a use of the expression 'words fail' then this is where it is applied, and this is the reason that the word design & the word conception are often used interchangeably.

Taking the chance and designing a product, in so many cases, is a total gamble. All the while wading into the murky waters, into certain uncertainty becomes the only manner with which the unknowable ever becomes the known. For individuals or of societies it is the same thing. Consider the notion of not being bothering with any of it, then it is for sure there is an oblivion waiting for all of us. This is where no one rolls the dice and nothing is ever achieved. To be able to determine anything that influences us or attempt to lay plans to things, that itself is over coming oblivion.

On the other end, we have the achievement of many known things. With too much knowledge and not enough care we may in fact blow ourselves up, and into oblivion. Without a doubt this brings us at least to the very edge of another possibility. This is one where we once again rise against the tides of question and technically work out our moments. Here we gain the control.

It was unavoidable the moment individuals first got up out of the cave and hence plied their will onto the face of many rocks. It was those who set the wheels in motion, the remainder of the equation was only time, a curious but quantifiable amount of time.

On the one side, not enough power, on the other side too much. This is a 'what we are dealing with', genies out of bottles sort of thing, this is design each and every day. It is our influence over environment, and just how tricky is the slope? In between lay the safe middle ground of polite, persistent and good design. Spanning together a mixture of ideas resulting in the classic residence of being relevant for a long long time we can develop ourselves safely. This is maybe why doing good things takes a while.

Chapter Seven–
Domain Alteration

In the discipline of environmental design there is an ever present emergence of what is sustainable design or in particular what is green design. These are ideas in an ever expanding realm of modern style where what it means to be responsible in our duties indicates making things better, more efficient than ever before. Within this we can reach as far over the scope of creating better spaces, managing integrated qualities on smarter devices while costing less to operate.

All of these features are within the umbrella of what it means to design the things we need to fit more sustainably within our natural surroundings, with good taste and less damage. In actuality this is slightly removed from the concept of design to modify our environment. It has not always been desired for humans to feel the need to recreate what is already natural, it is just that we have made the choice to do so.

Most likely it was a decision made some 10,000 to 20,000 years ago, with the notion to completely redo our nests. This likely to better suit the needs of our individuals & groups, as well as to update our sense of our selves. Until we reached this mental shift we were mainly tribal, and after we were essentially what we are today, modern humans.

In this view, the environmental design we have taken to doing has bridged all that we had yet attempted to make things into, one integrated city system.

Until we lived in the urban setting it was not entirely obvious quite what we were up to. Now it all seems rather obvious. Here within a certain scale of sophistication, complete with ideas of comfort and proximity, the beginning of a total win over the environment has unfolded. We awoke to the realization that we had recreated our domain. The leap itself was within a long series of turns and events, all resulting in some near organic intricacy of design overlay for ourselves, that of dense physical design.

The city itself is an invention, just as simply as art is an invention. But one could easily ask how were they truly ever avoidable given that people have a pattern of developing things & living together. Was there ever a case where the city was not going to happen, were we going to build communities with something else in mind? History suggests that the answer is a subtle no. It has been a reoccurring artifact that by each version of civilization which is headed out we have always chosen the village as our platform. Larger and larger each time until some event ruins them. This is evident even without possible communication of the idea. Humans it seems like the idea of the city and have a knack for making them happen.

Maybe this is because community is part of human kind. After all that is where the collision of all our ideas has been developed. This is perspective, where our own psychology is somewhat visible to our interpretations. It wasn't always like this though. Seen as a massive city Rome only had about 250,000 citizens, not quite the same idea as today. This modern version is something else. It is hyper-dense, layer upon layer of sophistication sewn together. It is advanced beyond our wildest dreams.

The Duality of Surmounting an Idea

If a particular direction was initially offered up to guide someone through a problem, a pathway that seemed clear at the beginning, then trial and error would never need to exist. Most undoubtedly it does, and for it the bulk of good ideas and great solutions, tools and man-made systems come out of it. Creating a product is a messy and time consuming ordeal. It almost always has been, maybe with perhaps the odd exception. This period where the growth happens is much of the *substance* of design as it has existed since the first human light-bulb experience.

It is very different, the creative process, from even the image of clarity, for one must use real materials and unseen mistakes in order to crack the egg. Many items, whether it is a hand tool made of stone or a hair comb made from plastic, seem simple enough at the beginning. But the inertia one designer must face to get that thing banged out of that material is often a long and arduous process.

This is where we separate the light-bulb experience from some hidden vision of an item. Is there ever a 'when the pen hits the paper' moment, where the end result isn't even known until the experimentation has already started. This is more likely the path of common products, as it is in many works of great art.

This is why it is more of a discovery process than a race to the finish line, simply because all of the facts are not yet realized in the beginning. Take Roman hydraulics for example. They had the right idea, they had the manner by which they would lift their heavy loads, they had the rams for which they would force weight against gravity, they even had the fluidity and hose idea all worked out. It was all down to what was missing, what insight they lacked that kept them from a phenomenal success. They chose to power it all with water, when what they should have used was something more viscous, something petrol based.

This is the kind of small roadblock that tends to prolong many monumental developments within a great idea. Perhaps if even some coincidence came along we wouldn't have had to wait a couple thousand more years for such weight lifting machinery. If one can coin a top down idea, this is what it would look like.

If the artist begins working and experimenting with materials but admits to having no idea where this is headed, then it is more the other way side of thinking. It could be called a bottom up idea. Perhaps relating this to unknown ideas helps work through the rough spots with sheer motivation. This may be a component of discovery, where some clever and unseen combination presents itself to the artist.

Insight? Is it a rare form of some bubbling up from the unconscious? Leading to discoveries that matter? This is the unconscious lending to progress, perhaps it is alone with instinct or feeling. This has to lend itself to the gradual surmounting of big problems through the adding up many solutions. Taking all that we know and putting it into one box, adding all those steps already taken, all those incremental pieces and experimental results and overall determination. These top down & bottom up methods each have an unknown meeting point where we find our breakthrough moments. This is a duality.

This joining is where unconnected products, such as a handle & an axe head merge into something whole. Bringing together the shaped head & wooden handle, now we get a refined tool. A link between what previously existed as 2 separate although finished items, hence modification and revolution.

The Shortest Path Idea

The notion that thinking and planning, when put under enough pressure, will often lead to the simplest and least apparent of solutions, is likely false. A simple direction means where some heading of travel works according to some idea. By this there should be little or no divergence. If such a path is laid out leading from one house, across maybe a large lawn and over to another house then it could make sense that an amount of walkers would stick to the given path. This is often not the case. This is a factor linked to the nature of the individual walker, whom makes up their own pathway across that lawn. Whatever the angle or wander from the first building to the second is not exactly knowable. What if it's a straight 2 minute walk between these homes? Chances are more or less that all walkers will stay on this initial path. But what if the is a 30° turn halfway? It is likely that at least a handful of those going between them are simply going to cut across the space, making it faster to get there. Maybe there is a network of sidewalks on this same lawn, what if it is complex? When these walkways were laid out there may have been a plan to keep people off the grass, how much allowance was there? With enough time, and enough walkers there will be new paths from various point A's to various point B's and there will follow patches of stepped on grass. It is human nature, and with fewer paths and a more complex the journey, the more side tracks will be made.

The logic is that there is little logic to just how many and which possible routes will exist. There will be common routes and less common routes, but all will occur just the same. This behavior is deeply nested in the traveller. It is really the same with design, a subconscious is unknown. It is for sure that at the end of the day there will always be some trampled grass along with unheard of ideas. Maybe it was not even about the shortest distance, but rather the most scenic walk between these 2 buildings.

The realization is that people are nearly impossible to predict, and much of what they decide to do is not even at the conscious surface. As are most things is integral to the idea developing process things will unfold however they may. This is a component of a much larger scene, that of creativity. Discovery is hard to predict. Knowing where things are going to go is basically impossible.

Great inventions are like this. They live inside of these ongoing boxes as much as they can and then they obey the almost random parameters in how they come to the light of day.

Sometimes the shortest distance is in fact the longest path. Sometimes it takes a very long time to generate a good idea. If in fact one is required to do a maddening amount of experimenting to come up with the answers then it seems long is still actually short. It all depends on the end result.

Chapter Eight-
The Psychological Gates

Psychology is our window for taking into account, all of the human to human relations. It is also a manner to see the diverse measures by which the person interacts with the physical world. It is a complex mix of variability & influence, where we can study ourselves in both a small and a big picture type of way.

As in our own deep history we have had a chain of self-effecting innovations. Of the variety within design and possessing ingenuity we have been all over the place. We can easily observe mainly the big picture stuff, but it is a little more tricky to comprehend the tiny adjustments we have made. Critical of the course set for ourselves along the journey to being modern man the small details have made at least as much difference. Adjusting for change, responding to chance and using alternative techniques helped the earliest of men and women piece together things a fraction at a time.

Cultural shifting has followed what we have made for ourselves, both with tool and trade. Carrying the society at large is within design, as it is with many crafts. Freeing ourselves up has been the job of the imagination combined with a little focus. Seeing original items made in ancient times is similar in that the outcomes were very large. It has been through those experiences that cultures and persons developed into what they are now.

The Ingredient of Madness

The imagination as it exists within many forms of possibility, loosening the bonds of conscious norm, is a way to change the world a little. Into what may then become fluid thoughts, an adjustment of what is usual gives into less familiar lines and new patterns. Artistry & art have to move around a bit in order to stay fresh and to test the limits of expectation.

A natural method of presenting what something could be like is perhaps a true form of reality. It comes to us without the limits of paradigm.

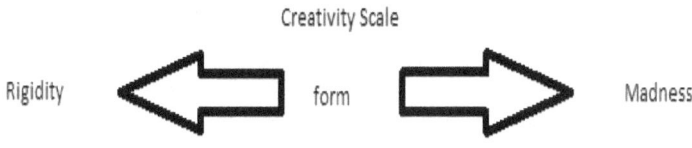

Fig 2: Creativity Scale

So it is honest design that has to be focused and obviously, in what it can potentially be, becoming purposeful as it adapts. Shuffling of what bonds apply to the thinking of what items mean to people is no different than fleeing the rigid and gaining some ground towards chaos and madness, breaking things down by sloughing off some small piece of the old, adding bits of the new.

The amount of creativity going into experimentation is a

little bit of the unconscious and some minute amount of the unhinged. Without breaking bonds nothing can ever change. This is how the carbon atom functions and how life gets moving, by constantly being on the move.

Art is skill through practice, application of creative skill or of imagination, or the works acquired by imaginative process. The more accepted the experiment is with the masses the more mainstream it will likely become. But even obscure products can become great successes. Some idea that seems totally 'mad, or the type that is turned out by a 'mad artist usually spends some of its life at the fringes.

The truth is these objects are often every bit as important, because eventually they are needed. To release one's work into the lime light and hence the known is a growth process all its own.

By having risk taking behavior and the talents of any person things seem to happen with great influence. Intelligence & risk are the main reasons mankind has survived this long. By adding a dash of madness we as a species have been able to turn the impending wheels of circumstance and shuffle the deck, sometimes towards failure and sometimes not.

This allowance for toying with the odd is part of our own psychology and our own internal methods. We have manufactured a game of chance out of thin air, this has been the story of human success.

Neutrality is simply not enough. To work without illusion or to avoid bad design, is the same as not taking risks. And big risks turn out some legendary designs.

If this method is powerful enough to define who we are in social groups or 'who we see ourselves as', then how can we get this without taking chances in our ideas?
Minimal, skeletal simplicity, that which is easy to understand, is also much about design. This is the essence of long lasting and broadly inspiring design. It is simple to digest and easy to keep around. And then we ask 'how is it influencing us'?

Becoming Psychology

The overall users begin to recognize patterns within successful products. Later, as these become more commonly seen, there begins to grow definition and feedback. We identify with these objects. Defined in such a way as to be partially unconscious, identifying with the connections of so many useful things gets personal.

As development seeps through invention (sine qua non) the picture gradually moves. The occurrence is a shift in ourselves. Designing form changes further plays with our identities. It settles time and again in different comfort zones as the product and society creeps forward. Products co-inhabit the reality of its people. The design intention itself has an outcome on who we are. It takes us all down a road which becomes our own history, shaped by what we make.

The raw degree of experiment takes this new shape, changing culture. This is the building by pulling on the imagination strings of free association, of free thinking.

There in is a process of manufacturing crafts, like stone axes or fire. It is after this that we are along for the ride.

Chapter Nine–
A Definition of Appreciation

Design or Legacy

Art does not have to be in any particular way functional, this is known through our endeavors into post modernism. We can have art, we can have its ideas without a certain functionality, that is not anything more than just what it is, something to behold. While this is a thought we still have design operating much separately from this, even in the opposite court of man-made items. While pretty things are often wonderful to look at we put designs into play because they do something past what they merely are, they serve long standing purposes. Perform functions which would otherwise not be there for us to step & use to benefit our day and our tasks. Take the example into just about anything, it must serve an almost ritualistic task for us to find value in it. Otherwise we simple toss the object & get ourselves one that is up to the challenge. This is the cruel fate we have given designers, update or be dispensed.

Art is not like this, and neither for that matter is architecture. We can have ugly buildings, we can have houses with no rooms or doors. Does this mean it is still a house at all. Perhaps, but then again this sounds more like sculpture or art, for it may again be just something to simply look at. Architecture must ideally serve some quantifiable purpose too, but is less defined by the hard set rules of say an escalator. Fancy pants structures go up all the time, and in many situations do not ever suit the setting where upon they are placed. Does that mean we up and tear them from their footings? No actually, nearly always we simply put up with them, as they are expensive and took ample time to put there. This is the difference between the 3, and yet they all exist around us and in our lives because of how they work and because of what each stands for.

By the same pursuit architecture does not have to break any molds. It doesn't have to reinvent itself every few years to stay relevant to our circumstances. Even several successful buildings we had made thousands of years ago are still standing with a legacy, still useful in purpose to us by simply knowing they are there. Here these are now statements about ourselves, 'yeah, we built that' and somehow we can still see ourselves toiling away with plans and bricks and stones. It serves a meaning for us, a span to shake the hand with ourselves, across all those years. Here we have a legacy value, this is more difficult to find with designs, but less difficult to spot in our art works. We can speak more to ourselves through a sculpture or painting than through an old coffeemaker or radio.

This isn't actually ironic, for we have designs without a certain spirituality, along-side us in our daily lives, almost empty cavities if you will. Filling tasks & need without the requirement of reflection upon them. This one holds a bit of spare change neatly, or that one dries my hair quite nice. We simply are not required to stop and appreciate their usefulness, it would actually seem too distracting, and would be a bit weird.

On the other hand architecture is not like this, we stop and appreciate it nearly all the time, it would actually seem a bit rude not to stop and take in the impression it gives us. We have entire University courses dedicated to this one aspect of our world, and why not, it pertains to the beauty we find within. Here is exactly what it ties together with art, an idea fulfilled, present in the physical sense, for us to stop and stare and take it in 'how does this make me feel?'

It is the ignored, the truly unnoticed, that is drastically unappreciated in our world of design. Our hardware stores are filled to the brim with such items, as are our streets and shopping malls. Designs coexisting and actually while facilitating other beautiful items such as fashion. This is the lovely set of stairs that gains us access to our favorite boutiques selling us high chic attire, all nestled together like cereal.

Unto this architecture has a choice to be either functional or non-functional. It does not have to push any rules out of the way in order to achieve what it has to do. In a sense as styles change or stay the same way basically forever, the ideas co-exist somehow, as long as things somewhat match, glass beside stone, aluminum with wood.

One must consider most of the non-functional makings as the natural discovery of artworks. As with our cultures this is a sink for our spare time, our recreational thoughts are placed here, considering things against the norm. It helps carry our imaginations and bears very little responsibility, it is beautiful this way.

But it has become design, as an event, which has obligation to break things and provide purpose, but to stick by our side and please never leave us. It has to come loaded with a sense of purpose, responsibility, with a focus or perspective of the idea, which we brought it to life. Design is very rarely nonsensical. The point of an item designed, is that it carries some activity towards its end point, it makes our lives better. Here exists its ever present ever occurring value. It can be borne at once, in itself with the act of making something possible, but it seems more quiet or polite somehow.

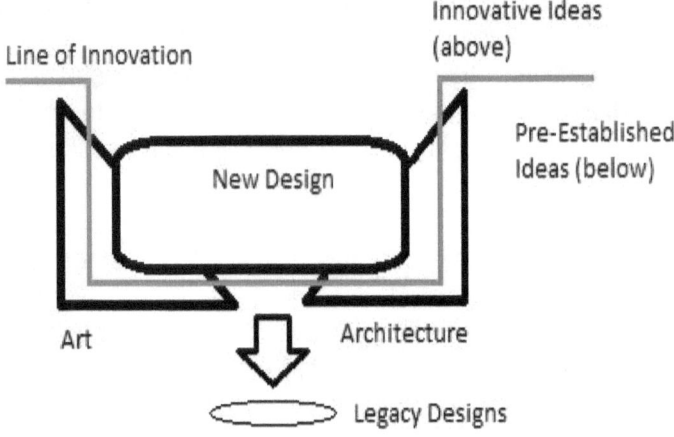

Fig 3: The Line of Innovation

This is a simple illustration to outline the 3 disciplines as change is dealt with. This alteration in constancy is seen as New Design, that which is always moving forward. The line is seen as the border between the worlds of new and old, of New & Legacy. Above the line things are like quick sand, always in flux or update. Here around the actual border are some of the areas which overlap. These share status between new and legacy, a blurred mix. Below the line is what is calm and ever-still, that where no alterations are desired. As can be seen some parts of art as well as some parts of architecture fall on either side. Where down at the narrow cone end of constantly shifting design is a piece of the action where all the best made things spend their lives just as they were made originally. The Legacy Design is for all art, architecture & design, it is the aspects of already well defined ideas that do not require any change to be just the way they need to be.

Chapter Ten–
The Deep Design Perspective

Pathways are much of what good storytelling consists of. It is the course by which end results are achieved, that by which we see and observe what is truly crucial. Here we take in the overall development in a life span sort of way, of both individuals and the means that lead them to some fruitful destination. Besides being these characters, residing inside their stories is all that an adventure consists of. This is what gives us our sense of participation, as if we were there ourselves, all along.

Consider the material of this capability that is a distinctly human ability to imagine a situation, to place our minds into the occurrences, this despite the time at which they actually took place. This mental movement, this fluidity of the self is the activity of placing the mind into something else at another time. There wouldn't be much going on without this for it may be the single largest talent we possess, as both individuals and as groups.

This is why storytelling and the simple act of listening maybe the most fun there is for us. These ideas bind us, for we can relate to both the story and to each other in our shared experiences. Having the capacity to relay the depths and meanderings of our great stories as we know them is much of what humanism is.

Creating this path is as much to be admired and relished as the re-telling. For much of our development is bound tightly, even welded to the singularity to observe and digest. But what would a story maker be without the absorption of detail. Having this tenacity, this candor to bring out a story in the first place, as anything that exists outside of historical rendition is some creative fiction. Development of the mind and the sharpness to present what one has digested and is ready to expose, this is the realm of the storyteller & the designer, as it exists separately from the artist.

Influential Mediator

It is in here that we have it, a slowly wandering definition, a noun, a verb a pronoun. In different generations the actual meaning of the word has slowly changed around, loosely describing the general. Within a modern day definition, a designer is someone who works out all the structural details of any one object. If we were discussing the 12th century and people working the kinks out of how to build stone archways, the parabolic type known as the roman arch, we would likely be talking about architects or masons. These are different descriptions at different times in history. Depending on the decade of the mechanics of the term, it actually takes on a different meaning.

The truth is the focus of things change over time, especially centuries. If it were the case during one era to coin the term architecture, then in all likeliness it is describing a different arrangement within another time. Overall it remains the broad like craft, but in the case of some the general craftsmanship begins to fall under different names. Even if by and large architecture has remained true to its far reaching description, it is within the more technical arts that we have a drift. In this it is what one is entailed to do within each craft.

If one were to take a longer look, into the beginning of people playing influence onto their surroundings, a mere term would suffice, that with which we can easily comfort ourselves, matching the doing of something with the words that fit. In ancient times it was the craftsman who picked up the first sticks & stones and made the decisions as what to do with them. But they certainly were not referred to as designers as we tend to think of the word. Those proactively affecting their environment, even technically, they had the ability to create. If it was art, or if it was social science, if it was architecture or engineering, it would be all the same to a cave dweller. But in some high sense, it was all design.

Design is this middle ground, but in many ancient instances, it would have encompassed the entire ground of creativity. There was much to do, and with so little yet done, the entire aspect of the undertaking of advancing man out of the cave took on a special meaning of the term.

For at that instance it would have been discovered why- would we bother working our way out of the circumstances we already had. Whereas today, this isn't even a question, no one any longer asks why or considers such thoughts, it is obvious. This is a critical difference, and one that underlies what Deep Design is. In a far flung world of our modern era, the term designer includes both tangible & intangible items, both concrete & abstract thinking. In the old world sense it basically was a description for anyone practicing a finer art. Today not only does it encompass technicians of sorts, but as well the list of what used to fall under artisan craftsmanship.

One big distinction is with our early-man, there was a void within what we now know as theory & training. None the less, objective items were given an evolutionary process, as they were shaped by the mind & the hand. Once the envelope for creatively making something had become open it was all progress from there on in.

This broadness of what was being carried out is a testament to individual knowledge, it is the deeper definition, and it is the seeds of what it is to make something. If the object is thought out well enough, it stands a good chance of taking shape and sticking around for a very long time, and being in the lives of those who created it.

Right there, on that place of sitting and in that place of discovery many thousands of years ago, as the outside activity took place more or less for the first time, we had discovery. All-encompassing ground work unfolding for future generations where a refinement took hold. Everything that happened between picking up the stones to shape the axe with blunt objects, to the braking of it while using it in the field, is the original path of design, the original step forward. This is the very first definition we have, and perhaps the very first human occupation there ever was.

Objects Surrounding Ourselves

Those items, those that makeup the spaces that surround us each day, everywhere we go, how much of that is man-made or man influenced. The chances are that a great deal of this material has been touched by human hands, and thereby a human mind and human determination. It is in the little items as it is within the big or less subtle ones. We have compiled some richness into our surrounding tapestry of our world with these intentions, the ideas we have built with.

Over large amounts of time, decades & centuries even the more natural, modified, or sublime of items, seem to house a blend of human minds because someone has molded it. Very old features of very old cities, old bridges and old pathways have withstood many elements. But whose nesting is within our own lives, someone, somewhere set about putting that item there, for various reasons and then seeing it influence us.

From tiny things to the large, indeed together carrying our realities, here we have self-determinism. It is the way our things work together, along with each other, both objectively & subjectively all at once. It is here, that we describe thoughts in the things, in our ideas, those which brought about literal result.

At certain points, we likely tried thinking in whole new ways. With societal success or failure our species pushed into its own determinism. If there became a way no one had ever considered thinking before, it likely brought with it a veil of the further possibilities. The likely hope would have been to decrease the chaos felt by those living in such times, and to hold some greater control over their surroundings, their lives and their destinies. They would have studied pattern, they would have studied symmetry, they would have considered cause & effect. In our modern sense these became present within every school of design, right from their establishment.

Grains of Perception

The birth of analogy perhaps was all part of the equation, to see something and to interpret it. Engineering mind? Designing mind? Discovery of the fine details, discovery of outcome, discovery of aesthetic relationships, an original & existing human island of thinking. All of this likely came in steps. Bringing together both the cognitive visual information and the social connectivity, the second leg of the journey began.

The cognition that grew out of this was the networking of different tribes as they inter-related with their new customized effects. This began reactive motion of ideas and change. Much of this is what remains today, as relationship is a birth mark of aesthetic culture and function. Even within schools of architecture and art it is the very idea of relating where things begin.

Deep Design vs. Fashion

For something to look good it does not have to work well. For something to take on some task with efficiency it certainly does not have to look anything but terrible. Items can carry on being ugly and maintain a relationship between form & function. Art does not need to function, it does such very well. As a purposeful object it does so while performing a zero contribution to anyone. On the other hand design does in fact need to carry out function, either specific or general it must give back some effective duty in order to exist. Oddly enough architecture does not really have to do either. It can take place, be completed, take resources and attention, all the while contributing neither good looks nor functionality. There are in fact several structures which stand as an experiment to this end, they as objects are completely redundant while being materially ineffectual.

Within what may be coined Deep Design, as the psychological earth beneath the device of invention, there exists good design. It resides here much like a theory, it has longevity as its main proof. Here, below the level of the aesthetic, it resides if one wishes to acknowledge it. If with the fine arts the soul of the work pertains to the aesthetic, it is design holding value, and Deep Design contains context amongst mankind.

Continually there is something much more discrete happening just below the surface. There is the non-appearing design, that of which it takes to piece together the tangible. As such it is the highly functional but the non-concrete of what made things happen. It is akin to an organized method. It is this that can operate free of rigidity or of fashion and at the same time does not require an end user's input. This is a form all its own.

If we view a marble figure of a person, then much craft and technique was poured into it to expose the shape out of the marble. Due to its resemblance to an actual person it takes little effort as a form of invention, although invention was required to make it, as well as the tools and methods needed to complete the job. Being a final item it merely describes what we already know, what a person looks like. But for this it needs next to no mental investment by the viewer to understand the piece, albeit most viewers could not carve the statue themselves. Still this is recognized but not to the point of detail. It was complex and time expensive to make.

In many ways this subtle non-appearing design is the perfect design. Where users simply do not mentally participate but physically use the object in play all the time. Objects have invisibly aspects, secrets unless called out specifically.

This includes deeply functioning items operating below, these do not require people's impressions. The joists in a floor, specific hand tools, motor pieces or engine parts, all working well while never being full realization of their importance, each of these items are subtle and could have been made in several different styles, each from unrelated origins, all performing just fine.

But to this they all include design effort and personal perspective, even intricate methods of thinking. In the outer world they are part of an invisible framework, free from aesthetic evaluation. A counter intuitive representation of design, it is the 2nd tier below the surface.

Chapter Eleven–
Projectile Process of Art

The Flight from Some Place to Some Other Place

The action, as it were, is a pursuit, although a blind one. It is the action leading towards something while abandoning something else, for some unknown outcome, an in-situ discovery of one's own creative trajectory. Within this lies a process, a leverage unto how to go about delivering the self through the material, to a point of landing, a later determined spot. This place, from a known departure point, the exact point of coming down to earth, where the craft is headed to is anyone's guess.

That path exists between the beginning & the end. It is an outcome with a 'there it is' type of arrival. With this a work of art is found in a moment, when and where it finally arrives. It becomes recognizable only then in its final form.

The journey of creative discovery, that which exists in all design, is a subtle process. It is one which must manifest in order fully declare a visual outcome. During the path of originating some work of art there is the burning question...just 'where is this going'....?

The thing about a javelin, once in flight...is that no one can know for certain exactly where it is going to find its mark and land in the ground. Every second that it goes through the air this becomes more and more obvious. Where it is not going to land does as well, but it takes the entire process to see the end result.

The Analogy of 'Pushing Thru'

This is the far distant end result of such a creative projection, the final discovery, the result. It comes about while transitioning within a living series of original thoughts. The habit of pushing through is where all meandering roads lead...eventually...to complete product. This is based on the true essence of discovery, as being born from a vacuous curiosity of 'where do we go from here'...an all-important query at any point in time.

Things in the process come to a point of a peak, where something previously had not been. Where-as before there was a blank space, like an empty piece of paper, now there is representation and sophistication, a full arrival of conclusion.

To get to such a point one must utilize certain aspects of focus in a most basic sense. One must have:

- Object to work on & tools to work with.
- The concept of what that object may become.
- Specifying distinctive details of what is as well as what isn't available to use with technique & tool.
- Applying possible method & technique to work out the initial problem with as much clarity as possible.
- Understanding that you do not know exactly what you are going to get.
- The following of intent until reaching limits of ideas.
- Being able to go beyond this into what is not known, into seeing how the process plays out, and visualizing where you may want it to go.

It is about process of visualization and of thought, having

an angle on a problem and being able to fully define it throughout the procedure of carving it out into a tangible form. One must specifically apply one's self to the problem until something fits the picture.

Masters of the Chaos

Into the vast unknown, this creative process pushes forward, never really grasping its own distinct power with its lessons learned. The hardened materials pumped out make a difference to everything which follows, both directly and indirectly. The distinction of control is hard to speculate upon, what is intentional, what is accidental? In between lays the bulk of how it happens, how the masters carve out results. This goes along what eventually leads to fastened rules, adopted techniques and first rate classics. It is what transpires in the murky middle while attempts are made to achieve well made products and admired results.

Control, where there perhaps is little known control, as the work of a test pilot, feeling out the way to keep the visual in the frame, ideas are brought into the light. Not losing focus for distraction, this is where art, design and technique overlap.

During the flight of the hypothetical javelin, if all variables were known and all equations determined, there could be still a small margin for error. Some element of nature may cause interference. Other than an accurate guess, to the final point of rest upon the ground, it is all simply unknowable.

Into this is the sample arc of what it means to create art.

There comes a further presumption that nothing will act upon the path of the javelin during its path, could it hit a bird, there may be rain or wind. Similarly the lines on paper or the smudges of images are the same as the chunks of stone falling from the marble.

Discovery processes test our basic control, our thin co-actions. Those that all bear small relationships with the general flight path and make the point of landing actual, small effects big result, just like art. This is the chaos at work. Where things are complex the destination is unknown, to both the object & the artist.

This is what is taught to us by our systems of creativity and by our tools. It is a slow manifestation, a narrowing destination. What we perceive may simply be an illusion. This is certainly a type of reality, one that does not suggest to us that certain objects cannot be made.

This is the fluid of the medium, that of art & design. There a complex roll of the dice, one simple arc, just like art itself.

Into a direction as accepting some interface to work in and adding our techniques we force our will. Artist carves out a destination from blank canvas or stone and we have a new reality. Creativity follows this 'push thru' process, a self-accepting give & take game of forcing forward.

It too happens as the visual perceptions are sifted through. As the item is being made the end result slowly comes into focus. While things happen, the revealing of possibilities occurs, while others are shed. It is all taking place in the *now*, in the interplay of the mind between object and artist.

As things unravel and paths determine all becomes known, everything takes shape. This is how things get laid down and made, the essence of the creative structure, as seen in design. It becomes history, and all that previously wasn't now is.

Something Isn't, Until It Is

Artists must continue down creative paths, construe unto thus...chase after it...claim it...into being...into existence. It is their deliberate quest. Follow it into making actual and tangible objects, and make things as real as real can be. This is why we, and in fact how, we come to realize that to actually *know* something – definitively – is to exist within it ourselves. To show that something *is* and that something *is not*, is possibly transference itself. This is the act of defining the art.

It is within this that one can begin to master some, if any bits, of the known chaos. Like taming the way we react within it, slowly, as one would act with a wild beast. Still not really being sure what comes next or even totally trusting it, we come to know thy-self with it. Little by little breaking the bigger patterns into individual mannerisms, turning them into their very own components, their characteristics & traits, so as to discover each tendencies.

As some new item is a combination of many of its parts there is an ongoing process that itself is not inert. It becomes formed from a picture of something specific. This is where it undergoes a process of elimination along its way. Things gain momentum and the image gains clarity. This is done by gaining control over the medium and by continuing to push it through to the end point. This is an overcoming of chaos and a manifestation of abilities. Perhaps as much as anything it is a type of self-control.

Chapter Twelve-
The Purpose of Design is...

Decisions

Making hard decisions, being decisive in moving forward, design is based on committing to transforming things based on firm decision making in tight spots. This is a means to moving ahead. It is a type of leadership, but one akin to the materials being worked with. Keeping with originality and its pursuit is often cut out by firm thinking & problem solving. Having the tenacity to keep on the creative trail within the parameters of the original idea often means making concrete decisions. Expelling features and shapes is along-side this methodology, not being timid to the point where things get tossed. These are each characteristics of successful design.

Obeying the Subtle

Little changes become big alterations, and can completely steer direction as products and projects grow up. Where small turns within the direction of a design heavily influence all the following possibilities that may be enveloped into its final form, each small tweak is usually taken under control of someone who has mastered the medium. Differences that make a difference is a slight bit of a mantra. Having the capacity to know what information these miniscule bits are based on is a sign of an excellent designer.

Asking Questions

Interactions of materials is an obvious one, as perhaps one of the oldest experiences of designers, learning how an interaction is going to play out between different physical contents is vital. If we are even going to examine the relationship between stone and bone we can confidently mention that the learning going on here has been around as long as people have.

Getting involved with the natural scape and experimenting on what is possible, is a base point of design itself, without trial and error there would be nothing to discuss. Enquiring minds have led the field since its ancient days, it has always been built upon a need to know and a desire to try things. One fundamental characteristic of humans is a quirk, the idea to make things easier to do. Whether this is a root of laziness or an attribute of efficiency, who is to know for sure, but in actuality the motion is relatively the same for the fact that people like to make tools and machines to make life of less work and effort. This is a deep compensation, one we have more or less built our species upon. If there is a clever analogy it is that humans like to work smarter not harder. We are also naturally questioning everything. As time moves forward it is designers who are constantly finding ways to renew & improve on the old, to remake the world we live in.

Doing the Experiment

As with so many things, making something requires a leap of faith, a little bit of belief. This has to be done, otherwise nothing ever gets done. Giving into the action of hands on material, even if directly from curiosity, gains us the experience we need to identify with our world. These may be cooperative or these may be resistant trials, they may be either dull or dangerous, but it is within the interactions that realities are found.

These are in fact slightly other than our human real world experiences, and these are what materials teach us, and how we learn to manipulate them. The materials of the world tell us what they can & cannot do. Here is the game of creativity. With much aspect as to the subliminal & small there is much success to be gained, all on the attention level.

To this we pay attention, it is our ticket out of the mud, it is the difference between useful and excellent. By this manner simple crafts are born into art. More of the mental aspect it is a process where we feel the behavior of the craftwork, we allow it to guide us somewhat, listening, watching, gaining the technique of what we wish to perform.

One part science, one part reality, one part sensitivity, it has all to be added together with the element of free thinking. Given the allowance to go in any direction with some design grants us an approach to problem solving not achieved by going through the motions. It is by gut instinct just as much as combinations of ideas never placed together before. A creative clarity erupts, not void of technique but open to mastering one. It is the essence of the human mind.

Big Picture Stuff

What then are we supposed to suppose, or what should we then make of all this, the creative fuss, the tooling around? Is there something to all this, or have we just picked up stones cause we had finally gotten rather bored of it all?

Profound declarations are inevitably mute of the point itself. Behold, all deduced knowledge, we are thus! Whatever the way the reality exists in either case, the series of inventions has happened. The art has been made, the structures pieced together, and much of it just in people's own free time. We are modern and in fact we are human. So why all the development, why all the bother?

Time's Anchor

The purpose of design is that it defines who we are, it explain us as humans, and what we are capable of. It takes a rather large imagination to reach into the cases of the past to see just how these had worked for us, as a way to see into the future, to see ourselves with a future.

It is able to, as imaginative powers are able to, see into the past as well as see into the future at the same time. It is a way to see ourselves in these components of time. It is an imagination that is required to look across history and accurately see ourselves having the same desire to see ourselves here in the present, as we look into that past. It is a window on time and is who we are as a species, with our mental aptitude of mind.

So here we are, in our own future, unable to recognize ourselves in the beginning, in the distant past, due to the largeness of the overall span of time that we have forgotten. It has been so long that we tend to not perceive ourselves.

Design is in fact also acting as time machine. Very early on things were made to obtain a future other than getting by with baby steps. Now we have that future, but we cannot remember many of the pieces of that puzzle. It has been faded from our identities, but this is consistent with the way our memories work. It is the process of just how creativity and change have been front & center for a very long time, constantly marching forward.

It is in fact the same as getting a job done. There, it is done if you will, forever in place, and by us it is complete in a very permanent sense. Here with us now for the long haul, the chair, the language, the tool, the song, we are now inseparable. It has been made and further has added to the largeness of the picture. There, now we have done it, we invented a part of the puzzle, now we can move onto the next experiment, and so on. Mark one up for the people team, a series of points if you will, as they manifest into our very own being & lifestyles. Eat some fruit or eat some grains and you are alive. Eat some toast helped out by butter and a toaster and you are a modern human, one with endeavor and bravado and a subtle hint of accomplishment.

It is a two way mirror acting upon ancestors and ourselves. We are built on them and as it turns out they were built on us. We likely also established the mental mirror, for they wanted to be us, people with a future. In truth they became us, & we are still them, it is simply an illusion this separation. We have in actuality spent a great deal of time considering one another through this reflection. We are here, you are there, we are us, it is psychological.

"It's important to discover that mistakes are often far more compelling than the thing you set out to do"

Marion Weiss

While setting out to find one place another is found instead, does this sound a bit like Columbus. Hard to separate the actions, large brush strokes often come by accident, but contain a similar intention. If you set out to make a cup and come away with a bowl, is it all that bad? Certainly not if you gained so many things along the way, you now have dish to eat with & now you understand how to replicate it. It is a strange thing, this discovery, but it is the spine of design intention.

Originality is an interesting idea all by itself. How does it come about? What do we think of it? Certainly it is a proven necessity to much of our industrious well-being, and many of our passions are based in it. But what can we say about it, about it and our desire to come up with it?

The prospect of discovery is very attached to feelings and insights, to a knowing that you have to get somewhere you are not yet certain of. As people we are built to examine things with a quirky eye, and to question things. By beginning with hardly only an inkling, solutions gradually come out, it's very much how these things usually happen with designs. Great things come from simple things, but development comes with both sense & analytics. It takes a human to come up with something new and forever useful, and much of the time it is a messy affair.

Transformative ideas take further time to develop, and often not all the pieces of the puzzle are known. This is something of 'partiality', where things begin as half of an idea. Progressive solving must be linked with a use of our intuition, with only some perspective on the problem. When things are incomplete, but are along a process of finding something as a way to rethink a design, it means there is still work to do, as in many steps to take. As with the axe, each the blade & the handle had to be developed separately, before they could be forever combined into an everlasting tool.

In order to really change something some risk-taking is involved, which will need to be overcome along with that partiality. With such an approach there will inevitably be some gain of 'knowns' before the whole thing is said and done, before finding a whole & complete design. This is what separates discovery/design as an art form from design as technical work. A new way of doing things is being configured and is an adding to a complex challenge. This also takes place within shifting or drifting parameters, perhaps hunters must start to predate animals in trees, if there is nothing to eat on the ground. This is maybe the sort of method that relies on feeling and perceptions more than routine. With making something original, there are still missing elements, even methods, but the item will possibly be worth their effort in order to make something possible that before was not.

Discovery allows us to be free in the middle ground of the imagination, in a pursuit of what is possible & what seems fitting.

PART II

NATURAL THINGS

The Natural world possesses its own design language, that of how things are formed and made, and our actual memories being ruled by this. There is much exploration left to do if we are to fully understand how memory works, and just what role emotions play within them and within our experiences in life. Within this work is a basic look at how art relates to our memory and patterns of many things. We make links as humans, these are connected to the organic, and how we relay and relate what they are about.

Introduction-
Perception

An idea has value when it is put out there with the capacity for others to see it and understand it. For this to occur it must become packaged and delivered across both time & space, leaving it at the fingertips of the perception of others for their consideration. In order for this to occur there must be an image, one created upon a type of canvas that which is to be the medium, that which allows it to transcend time.

Not just simple bits of information, but encompassing well rounded thoughts, put into some type of form, if that is writing, or if that is architecture. The presentation of a message, the passing along of it from one person to another, has to become constituted somehow. Every message needs some method to get it there.

Art is like this, it is of this nature, where the contents are delivered to others by the way of a medium of the artist's choice. An allegorical understanding is upon us when viewing art, such as painting, the non-verbal representation of a message, can best be given through a figurative nature in art. Any social side of us needs a way to see this, the contents, the language with which it was made. This indirectness is of a psychological domain, it pertains to the inner workings of the brain & of our mind. Is there a fine line to draw, linking actual intellectual process or even biological process & artistic image, can we draw a link from how an image is made to how it is remembered? Yes, somehow in some aesthetic way. Art itself is based on perceptions requiring literacy, by the participants, to

110

make it work, it is finding it useful as well as emotional, in order to grant overall meaning and be stable in a memory.

Putting things together & forming them into items that are useful to more people has a larger influence on society in general. The externalization of messages, such as with architecture, sculpture, music, verse, writings, or works of art are the form & are the medium by which they are conveyed. They are forms, they are how they were thought out, they are the actual materials, they become the functional means of their own existence, and they work because they are human.

The abstract nature of a form lies in a nature that is not quite physical, and it is not quite abstract either. Imagining puts a face to what is the flourishing of the mind, when a picture is formed it comes from our perceptions. Once there it tends to stay. Here exists a realm, one of meaning, one where actual and personal details fill in the atmosphere linking us to the emotive content of our experiences, it applies to and we place ourselves within the memory with our own pictures. Conceptually concrete but physically not there, it is only a representation. Any actual ideas of how we place art & message in our memory bids a thought to what it is we see or what is our experience. The interchange ability of the perceptions of what messages exist behind a work and the art itself becomes built into what the viewer will 'know' and is in a dialog between the artist and audience. This is the functionality of intellect and it has a solid basis in our emotional selves, it is the access point of thoughts we contain about our memories.

An entwining of the senses is contained in experience.

Nearly free of any bias is the emotional history we create, have, or adopt during an interaction. It is clean and it is the way we have placed it within our memories, this is thought provoking. One aspect is that we can further look back at our past and re-visit the emotions, often with intensity. Another thing is that we create how perceptions go into our memories, this based on just how much feeling and individuality was present when something happened. After this is the content that is relayed in art, the culture with whom we are amongst, and how this affects our reading and our meaning of a situation even of past creativity.

Interpretation of the messages contained within art is through & based on the literacy of the reader, where after a span of time the artist can give the same meaning of a work of art to anyone just by using their ability to pick up on allegory, or the form of how it has been conveyed. It will transcend time and it will distort, and after such the message is not only based in the medium itself but on the reader as well.

The placement of a contemporary importance or an impact put into a message does not guarantee it a use later on. It does not promise it a future relevancy. Design integrity meets behavioural psychology as well as society, where things need stay pertinent over generations.

It is a proper representation that we seek, the already used language of the art itself and the ability of the viewer to read it, as presumed by the maker. This develops into a literary form, it sets the ground rules for the art itself, what is its purpose & what are our perceptions of it. When this develops into an emotional language it substantiates ideas to people, complex connections between artist and purveyor, who never will actually meet. Placing a weight onto these personal aspects of feelings in memories while in the experience of art, architecture or music, constitutes them more or less as an experience to remember, one that is more or less emotive.

Virtualization is the theatre of qualities people put into what they see. Unto this is also a cultural continuum, one which possesses a language of its own. There is influence in how an image can be given a message, time after time to a certain group of people. The environmental content has to be built into man made objects, there is a forging of purpose within what we use as individuals in our everyday life as well. Our experiences become loaded with memories and are transposed onto the object, which are inherent in this cultural pool. Our minds are our human platform, they digest as well as create designs and solutions in our world.

"the great scientific truths are similar to artistic images"

W. von Humboldt

Emotions have the capacity to bond memories to our everyday understanding of the events in our lives, forever tied into a relationship that connects to the way we observe things and live them. It goes into a space held between the outside world and our inner one. Here mental images come alive at whim, existing themselves quite free of concrete form, they are placed here, suspended &

mentally embedded. These items survive time and they continue some relevance personally and culturally.

What remains important and what allows us to identify any series of objects within larger groups has to become related to us and what we do. The character of things as they become involved with our memory helps explain an ontological gap which is some knowledge of meaning more than of property details. The overwhelming aspects of the world around us, even those of the abstract, contain much of the virtual items which are remaining, such as ideas.

Chapter Thirteen-
Design Psychologica

Within our everyday lives we are surrounded by items that we have made by ourselves, things that took considerable thought to create. Our cities and our cars, our gadgets and our homes, all extensively thought about and put together. The connection between a particular manner of use and the sharing of a function associated with it exist in a mental space. It is a conversation amongst methods and meanings held and used to fulfill the purpose of an object, how to read something, or how to use it.

Design happens within the normative culture, it happens within our lives. It has to remain intact in order to form the designated behaviour, the purported relationship, as well as sustain the nature of its parent cultural norms. These parents define our identities, they place relationships unto our own day to day selves. In a way that people may estimate what their experience of something may be when it happens, the causing of emotional preconditions, the user adopts these parameters even without knowing. Whether it is from a painting or a roller coaster ride, how does initial behaviour of someone set up the connection one will have with their memories. The nature of this is multivariate & the strands of which are too dense to really trace. Any language must take this into consideration, being aware that how a person feels and how they react also relates to them remembering something.

Are things long lasting, are images durable, are they safe from fading over time, are we sure about them? These become modern criteria of societies as objects we interact with must maintain some long lasting relevancy in our interaction with them. Within this is aesthetic value, overall form & function, content and of course purpose, either abstract or real. Matching, fitting or placing the specific needs of those who use these things, the nature of congruence, allows those descriptions of identity and the identifying with objects, to develop.

Agglomerations are groups, essentially larger masses of items all bunched up and functioning together in some way. They are separate from inanimate objects in that together they act as large bodies affecting the individuals within. Imagine societies or populations. Design must measure as a barometer does the inflections upon people that will be contained within the nature of how things are made. The behaviour of individuals comes out of the total meshing of cumulative cultures of works, they have helped in the creation of an image of a people, what they are like, how they act, what they remember & what they do as individuals and as groups.

Meshing together groups of ideas gives rise to cities and its people. A contact comes about in the way individuals experience a piece of architecture, or a piece of art. If it becomes accepted, enjoyed, used. The way citizens feel about an article of design as their human identity takes it on or takes it in, by this a relationship is formed. Any timeless quality present in design maintains social connection and contains the intent of its designer in a way that meets the expectations of differing people. Their thoughts and their feelings of what something ought to be like. This is a communication, one that associates and involves the study of groups and of design as being as important as the methods which devised it. The intention of aesthetic groups of things is to simply form connections, ones that resist fading, ones that are unique. These become the qualitative aspects held within the memory.

The language of what is communicated may be dense in its delivery, an artistic or design style takes time to establish, even if it exists solely in a simple chair. Functionality is solving problems one at a time, trying to keep them in their simplest form in order to give them subtle lives. Blending things in with our surroundings is of a certain school of thought, a certain mental frame to replace problems with enjoyment. We have become part of an establishment, where the intelligence required to engineer our stuff has started describing certain attributes about ourselves, our desires, our lives. In a general sense we make the complex into the simple, that is our desire.

Rethinking takes time, consideration, resources, it is a kind of attunement on transforming our stuff into a replication of the natural, the organic. We attempt a type of control within our stuff a, confidence of sorts. Our products it is hoped, are tightly constrained, yet inspiring, sophisticated, yet simple to use. We like our things emotional, and we also like them timeless. The image, the reflection that is supposed to bind well with a long term understanding of ourselves, it is supposed to be informative. We are ideally learning from the items which we make. The psychology of our stuff, as it embraces us, encapsulates our perceptions & allows us to see things in a certain way. Complicated things made easy – is the preoccupation of the engineer, making them smooth and seamless – the job of the designer, not to mention trying to make them fun. The appropriation of functionality has to reach a level where it appeals to some sense of the end user, either with convenience, solution, or raw emotion. They can include the ability to make people smile. What we get back from items is why we have designs.

Cultural inclusion is a more difficult issue. How things fit in with what is already established, if so desired, is a means of longevity, both for the item and for the people, those in society. Giving to and not taking from, becomes both the makeup and the value of social groups. The purpose is to make things better for, and not to replace people. There is no ambiguity in quality, nor in how people feel after things are made & put into society. There comes a growing understanding of how we relate to and use, what we make, & are appealed by them. How well we make things relates to our view of society.

How to avoid reducing value? This is something like environmental design or qualitative density. What do we think of skills and of craftsmanship, what do we think about our inclusion of our own selves in our stuff? Where do we fit in with all of this, once it has been made? The broader based solutions fade quickly, shorter more dense thinking employs a specified capacity of a product, where it fills a purpose very well, and has a place amongst a complex need.

Nature has a capacity to overrule the unpromising, a way to counter the redundant in short order, it is part of the ingenuity of distribution, of networks, catastrophe & of diversity. It is the self-balancing, it is the self-similar. Within all of the vast numbers as in members of groups, there exists an ability to attain answers to complex problems. Like with the averaging of things, finds their target by shear number. It is a capability to refine searches for things across networks, with rather great speed.

Groups of any kind, bugs, trees, ants, schools, by doing experiments, more often than not the same solutions are found to occur quite simultaneously, even in different places. It is an assimilation of development, which shapes cultures, & further makes ourselves. This is a rudimentary trait of nature, it can be found practically anywhere. Our understanding of functional attributes is not universal, it is our knowledge of how things are locally useful that is rather more important & accessible. Adding our complex and nearly ubiquitous understanding of beauty raises a deeper relationship. Nearly everyone finds beauty in the connections surrounding us.

How could we have, as groups, cooked up an answer to what is beautiful? The truth is, design is emotional. There is a very real chance that nature is also somewhat emotive, as adaptive, as learning.

Chapter Fourteen-
Redefining Personal Space

All within a few short years the picture had changed into a mild vision of what the future was to behold. With it, would come a simpler view, one that would be capable of clearing out vast tracks of confusing details, now pushed into the realm of the redundant, void of any value. This happened when the algorithm was married with evolutionary theory & it became something of a paradigm shift. Whereas the whole of an entire group of an interplaying population (genotype) differed from the actual individual players (phenotype) there was non-the-less a calculable estimation for the behaviour of groups. Much of the notion lay in a reactionary world of quantities, thought to be behind the computational roots of relationships. Even if human, those were to be based upon automata, but the way they worked together in large groups still seemed a far stretch, for some unknown reason.

> *"things should be made as simple as possible, but not simpler"*
>
> Albert Einstein

In life there exist expansive amounts of what is measurable & what simply isn't. What is natural to someone or the group they belong to is making a choice between what pieces are important and what ones are not. If what happens is always fairly constant than why can't it simply be measured? Well, this is the dead end for many social science experiments, because things aren't that simple at all, once they are in groups. Groups act in highly unpredictable ways. As clusters of elements match up together their overall behaviour and their image is altered. Knowing the parameters, some characteristics or even the functionality of agglomerations helps us to understand them, but in a limited sense. Our selves & our bodies of creative work, our social links & our relationships, all surmount to characteristics. Abstractly or specifically, the bodies always add up to something, more than numbers.

Memory, and more so human memory, exists & functions in an unfathomable space, one where the human mind has limits to understanding. With both average and not so average years of our lives, what sets all the pieces apart from one another? To what process do we owe the stirring of long forgotten things, from a simple glance at an object, to how we arrange our precise & pictorial memories within it? Particularities of items well remembered come not by simple list making, but is a highly human ability. Autobiographical details of our lives, the human condition and the arousal of much of what makes us up as individuals are forever entwined with the feelings that accompany the knowing to the parts of our own personal puzzles. Our ability to sense out what is constantly happening all around us each day means that there are fast track ways to absorb endless details, to swim within all possibilities. The learning of ever-vaster aspects of ourselves, from personal traits to functional characteristics, there seems something more malleable than a broad quantity of connections, there exists even a perspective. Actual view of our personal world makes an encompassing focus unto our own psychological well-being and upon just what we see when we are presented

121

with artful things.

The diverse is something we have all learned about, and generally, it is seen as an important trait, occurring everywhere in nature. It would have been some sublime clarification early on, that our lives each seem to work better within the condition of diversity. It practically cannot be determined to mean too much else except to describe a healthy ability. It would be simple then to understand that reducing and then isolating would come at a cost of the overall body of individuals, even of its objects as relating the details that are immersed within them, & would only suffer from simplification. More of the focus on overall process would allow more explanation as to the methods of larger groups, their behaviour, & their complexities. Social groups act as clusters of interactions, ever seemingly able to take on lives of their own, heading in directions not ever foreseen. Behaviour as it happens to be, is exhibited by sociologic dynamics, and where we are social creatures of habit and as most of what we learn comes in groups, and how we play off of one another is central.

Within our social surroundings a need for stability exists, where big changes are met with overall chaining of events, functional & changing connections play into the bigger picture. Each similar link is also tied to ever smaller relationships. Those amongst individuals and those between groups play a similar importance in how things end up being, growing or developing, as the many little details can force their way into the outcome of events of all kinds. Even if we poorly understand the patterns, those shaping their importance, we do get that they both exist and that they do matter. Even if prediction is quite out of reach there are mannerisms to each flow of exchanges. Whether they are between people or even molecules, they are there and always influential. It is a basic knowledge, a qualitative look into the things that are us, surround us & become us, where we gain a better understanding of design.

Better than odds

There is certain behaviour, that of incompletion, which rears its head in our world. It pops up in things such as earthquake patterns and electroencephalogram data, and makes a mark in much of what is important to us. Many of these breaking series of events lie in natural organization, when things actually work in groups. It is merely a human expectation that activities will occur in full and not in partial.

Our experiences are shaped more by fragments of a larger whole, mixed and matched into a fabric as in the compositions of music or a conversation. As you listen it becomes easy to notice many elements have been molded together, rather seamlessly, in the building of a sound event or in a song. Cultural expectations have us listening to entire and complete melodies, but each has been assembled as if glued together. Actually hearing music that is incomplete allows us to witness the pieces separately from one another.

The putting of pieces together and placing them into some auditory language, as observers, we are more used to the final process. If audio tape is spliced into a smooth functioning grammar than to us it becomes natural, it becomes music. The parts within each sound all have an individual existence and do function separately, they explain what modification may alter them into. Placing these entities side by side, as if they have borders that separate one form another a melding occurs, where separating lines disappear. Even if in a song their borders are never fully distinguishable they continue on within the larger body of sound.

Within the actual form of this whole come the bones of what it was made from. Important to the overall character and assembly of the style of sound desired comes the presentation language, the genre or mood of the music, the combinations themselves that stake many possible outcomes.

It underlines a truth of how things are further broken up even after some formation, what they can make as they are formed into something. It is an architectural space which must be defined completely, where music relates structurally. The actual remix is itself a process of nature, in how spaces are filled and refilled over time with forms, it really gets into a changing of possibilities. There is a connection between the inside and the outside worlds, a common realm is something being 'like' itself in perception whether on canvas or in music, bricks or tissues, there is an assortment of form as something develops. Common traits bind these in purpose, a putting of them into a larger relationship, giving causal and formal abilities to that form. Like memory itself, music & architecture each have their own unique assemblies & amalgamations. Its own pieces must be made functional, as the body of it belongs to a purpose.

Random sounds do not actually ever represent any music, as with details without any context of a whole are simply meaningless segments. This escapes the makeup of computers & data, for people are the essence of composition. The actual making of nature's building blocks into successful bodies plays out at a rate far better than some equal odds. By this there lives a bias, a gross tendency for purpose rather than failure, there is process in relationships. The development & mutations in behaviours comes to depend on influence, this is a sense of interacting parts & it is defiant.

The ways we put together our cities and communities often plays on what importance of connections exist and need to keep existing. Placement of parts does relate to the memories and the ties of both purpose and aesthetic. In our minds, our buildings, our parks, our streets and our addresses are uniqueness contained by brand. They are all massive, yet hold small patterns, for this is our means.

Our memories are tied to this process somehow. Personal history has experience of relationships, of our own linked with that of other people, this shared palette is much like a song, in a composition, in character, and has a medium in which to form.

Embedment in Style

Architecture has the visual burden of being part of our lives, shaping us, pausing us, reminding us of who we are, making us realize the passage of time. We are amongst all that we design and all that we build to enhance our lives and our societies, and yet are subject to it. Any & all devices of a populace can be carried into the future, all a matter of intended functionality of these items for us. All the spaces we occupy have present meaning, as do the sounds we are used to hearing, as in music. The shared assimilations are threaded together in each situation, we adhere to our senses and perceptions. Definition is provided by the value borne into the items all around us, upon this, what inherent patterns make the slight differences for us, in form & function? Cities themselves are nothing new, we occupy them, we make them communities, we marry them to our needs. Two aspects makeup the study of forms and what they mean to us, within discussing what people create.

Both artist & patron must fill the setting itself, enlivening the urban space, placing intrinsic qualities in our surroundings. It is perception, which drives this functionality, making it into something more than atmospheric and less than permanent. The human factor is the cultural culmination of many aspects which we have learned & exists in the places that we live. The patterns that educate us, live within us, even after structural things are dissolved and over. What do we make of this architecture, why is it a very human thing, and why is it so much more than conceptual.

Vienna had psychology, music composers, societal influence, grand architecture and placed importance on creating public knowledge spaces. So much more than a city it has given birth to vast tracts of fine art & self-discovery. Devising public space, places to expand on the imagination and the details encompassing our everyday thoughts helped to define just what Venetians thought of themselves. An actual representation of their places was made out of paying attention to a relationship within what people thought of forms and openness, of growth.

The initial manner of thought helps spur the curious, the inventive process, and our inner abilities. Ideas begin in the categories of facilitation, these inspirations left for us by established languages of art & design. What makes something of use to other people has a root within what its purpose is, and how a language has been developed to contain indirect information within it. Art is a form of this transference of a moment across time, containing aesthetic information. It has all been sequestered to capture something usually quite difficult to hold, ideas of our own perceptions.

What then would become of a global association, a conscious relationship almost with its own words. The what, in which we see where and how we materialize our surroundings, contains also the art & the experience within it. People have capacities for both inside & outside of a situation, within an experience, or as a test of the inner workings of thinking patterns, and their tendencies. How the outer world unfolds happens at the same rate as our conscience is able to deal with it, but contains no timeline for how we think about things and what we desire from them. There is often a loaded meaning in art, it has parameters guiding our thoughts, given essentially by our own experiences of the world and ourselves in it. Because so many people share similar perspectives with the language of art itself there is a large context to thought, a common one.

"the synaesthetic world is the world of colour, forms, sounds, smells and tastes that have all merged in an event to become a sensory toxification of form and memory."

R. Murray Schafer

In the environment of the un-measurable, it becomes value that which makes up the models of how things happen. Cultural creativity out of the chaos is a qualitative notion, nesting on the fringe. It builds and grows into the centerfold as all possibilities exist initially. There are universal associations of artistic image, when the accomplishments thereof cannot be quantified, it's the subjective through the objective. At the outset a bias can be made, with the imagination seeking a foundation, more through form than within detail. Much more examination of a whole can in fact be placed in this realm, within our transposition of what we see in a creative norm, this is still out of our literal understanding. Putting together what we see as important into finished products of art & functionality, we work as only people know how, just beyond the world of the concrete.

Music as Design

"ar" (art), Sanskirt; to join or to fit together.
Music is a place that often exists away from reality, a safe place for the ponderer and the dreamer alike. A soulful and easy access space where all you need to play it is an object of sound, an instrument.

Places where the mind is allowed to exist easing the pressure or limits of daily tasks has at any time a container of what can be made endless. The fitting of things in with other things has a more free flowing capacity, one with which sheer experimentation is allowed. In musical form a growth place, a rhythmic Cinderella is given as a starting point for all that may later find its way into the literal world, that of recordings.

Here a sound may or may not fit into a larger group of other sounds, but can exist for it is elevated in our thoughts, a non-interfering position where the fabric of the music is allowed to bounce around until it settles into a home position. Either amongst the capacity of our own mentality or now days within the world of software 'processing', a sound can find its own image and be married with others of its kind. All of this assembly can be molded into something else from which it originated as well.

Alteration and filtering of source sounds gives the world of transmutation of sound. A sort of genetic fluid of the identity with what noises had in their beginnings. Making things fit into a larger fabric, with each piece further drifting the sound itself away from its own origins. Something is created where before no things there existed. The systematic modifications which make them now suitable for their parent forms into a melody, a rhythmic chemistry, a song, is a composition. Distortion, delay, reverb, stretching, clipping and copying are all methodologies perfected by studio apparatuses in an effort to further control the destination of music itself. Many source type sounds are filtered within a battery of alterations, and even though they remain the same as an item of their own beginnings, they are usually not very recognizable upon assembly. Multiple items are to become combined into a slurry of indistinguishable parts & smoothed over through processing, to the point that which finding the boundaries of the initial pieces as roots becomes rather impossible.

All of the engineered sounds are placed into an overall sound event, where each item will lend itself to a whole in a very original way. Music is often chalked full of original events, characterized in a texture to form a relationship with those listening. With an audience not aware of when and where the first pieces had their changes an actual distance is formed whereby the sounds themselves are given a new beginning with those listening.

Orientation is linked within our usual tendencies of memory, a simple bias usually unclear even to the individual. Much the way our memories continue on what does a sound event eventually become after years of standing as an event? The quick formation into something which possesses a tone, a harmony, a melody, a persona, must form into something with function and longevity. How many people will it affect?

Putting things together in this way is a very natural action. It is something qualitative and is housed in our creative selves. What these source sounds were and how they live on is tied to the artist as she or he transposes them into larger bodies of work. As with a painting an artist's feelings shines through, becoming portrayed as a composition comes together, and is passed on within the work itself. Is it the same to stir emotion as it is perspective, in a sharing, a melting pot where the viewer is given the controls? When the event itself is becoming, and being listened to equally, it possesses a universal language where it leaves one aspect of the creative event imprinted to all, it has presence any time later on.

The medium itself can be shaped to reveal the direction of the composer, the idea given in a set of work that is more than a physical embodiment. A piece of architecture can make the same statement, as music it can begin to reveal emotions.

"a general consensus amongst the (lectures) about the need for embracing aesthetics, embodiment, presence and the non-reductive nature of experience as the starting points for a new philosophy of subjectivity."

Art & Identity Symposium, 2010

It is not a matter of picking items of favourite, or of preference, it is that so many items, music, art, structures, sculptures, whether we adore them or not, can be understood by basically anyone. To read the placing of ideas and aesthetic content, with meaning and context, within products is easy from person to person. Ideas can be purveyed into art, and their makeup can transcend time. By this they will continue on and influence countless persons, even if they are not popular.

Giving art a critique is to merely recognize it and be aware of its existence, once art is seen, heard, felt, it has a bearing unto society, it has a life of its own. Placing ideas, perhaps even in the curve of a building, allows an

131

approach of a viewer when noticed. It becomes merely an invitation to explore something laid out for anyone to see. To witness what has gone into the characteristics of something man made is to look behind the design and see the roots, as they leak into the future. Much of our imagination continues to exist out of the present tense & explores out of a time context. Memories will persist in links and associations however possible. Music can place images, being just one such medium utilized by wax or tape. It will maintain its composition for as long as the form exists. The songs which lie there for anyone to partake in, reveal their secrets, that being the way it continues to make people feel.

The canvas itself has many appearances, but it is always a human face behind it, & it is always more than what it looks like on the outside. Is memory a formation or something more biologically collected?

Profiles

As everything, everywhere, cannot sensibly all happen at once, there is an enduring time line to all things. A disassembly of complexity, the panning of view, gives each event more space. The placement of emotional experiences, one next to another in our memory, allows a bodily appearance. Aesthetics are part of a continuum of our relationship with outer things, but it is out of this that a language exists. Such as when we examine a painting, there are things we recognize in it that seem to come out of it and into us. It is an emotional communication based on previous understandings, memories, now making new memories. Art acts in a way, like a mirror, it causes external events about us, even if as simple as a discussion. Music allows us to capture our inspirations and to equally share them amongst ourselves. Architecture as same is able to reach out and touch someone, the many of us. In this way art is an act of influence.

Any of the micro-aesthetics within sounds can have a structural form, such as of loops. The nuances give compositions an aspect of space & texture. If such spatial qualities become gestures of a song then they are referred to as effects. These expressionistic gestures provide character and individuality within sounds. This is the chance to add layers & also is a way to provide depth to otherwise very simple noises.

Matching traits together makes sound form, present also in art, the combinations are ideally smooth and give presence to the overall body. There is both a positive and a negative space in the music, as in art, what is silent also provides definition to what is actually within the music, adding space and further body. This is a neutral space that unpacks, or cleans up the sounds that are meant to have room to provide the intended emotive features. The boundaries are structural & contextual, room to fit in with the overall body.

The beginnings of each work of art is infinite, potential further narrowed down as each choice is made as what to add. Mistakes themselves all have value, they become used and modified into some type of creative and unexpected fit. This is much of the Dub genre of music, as unintended characteristics become building blocks of a song. Changing each piece into a malleable and fluid match, unto the others surrounding them, creates both the timing and mood of a song. The message of what the audience gets out of a song is based on a spatial emotive conveyance of the music. This becomes over time, broadly understood by its listeners. An unintended path to completion of a piece of music is based on a mood and the purpose of artist, although just how this comes about is not predetermined. Establishing a piece takes it in a process of assembly, where it becomes put together and formed into something useful.

Chapter Fifteen-
Profound Networks

Just how is it that we get from dirt, to a whole tree? In some hypothetical discussion of what it would require for a healthy and mature tree to grow from water, dirt & sunlight, we have to consider its organization. For trees are not turned out of mere resources, all aspects of growth must become married into an organic form, somehow. Even if it were that trees are, by some chance, unrelated to most other natural things such as the brain, there is still a pending need for explaining patterns. Natural bodies, as they start, still relate to some evolved successes, and our ideas of biological beginnings are married to those of the self-organized. The capacity to relate to how things are locally self-assembled into larger wholes without a pre awareness of that whole, has networks imprinted all over it. A body with its connections is an entity, a collection of local physical components, and something that acts in unison. Emergence is our basis of understanding for when something becomes greater than the sum of its parts. It contains a character of a whole & is influenced as local parts communicate with global parts. Biological or not, systems exhibit unique behaviour amongst their own elements. This shines a light onto the aspects which are sewn together in the making of a tree.

How things grow in groups, larger than what they started as, is an exchange, a sharing. Many different forms act in a similar way, and it is important to consider just how complicated they can be. Even the simplest ecology is still a very complex one as there exist so many relationships, those that are relied on by the organism continuously. The given amount that an individual species is dependent becomes part of this web, a maintenance, a stability, a need, it describes embedment. The more outgoing influences an individual has, the more dependent the other species are, plant, animal or otherwise & needs do arise. This is how systems grow to balance themselves.

Successful influence begins to grow as a materialization within some surroundings, the quality of the change isn't merely about sustaining life, but fitting in amongst it. In the predicament that massive alterations are ushered in or become required, some very embedded species are uprooted due to the sheer amount of reorganization. Outgoing & incoming influences are amongst all the pieces of the ecosystem and in any group, biological or not, mutation leads to change. In a critical way, our trees wish to avoid this pressure as they are settled into a way of life. As in the history of Australia, when herd animals along with rabbits were put on the land, it crystallized a new ecological way. These inter-exchanges of relationships came about suddenly and had far reaching results. Diverse natural networks employ mutation as a way to select variety, and at any rate it proves very useful. It becomes the characteristics of a group that avoids the pushing out of a fit within one's home. This becomes problem solving, one that can withstand the stress of the orientation exchanges. As changes begin to embed and the new normal develops, a system comes into a new balance, withstanding this pressure can be a matter of creativity. Solutions are needed, the actual fit isn't a simple natural selection, it is more sophisticated than that, for it is self-determined. These new correlations themselves may be co-mutations of neighbor species, each benefiting from each other. Integration of this relationship becomes the center behaviour, not just the change itself. It is systemic.

Entire new ways of communicating can be molded out of sweeping changes. In total instability, there is opportunity for a broader foothold for a group. The tree itself can be described as a collective within a larger group, that of a forest. Much is known of what transpires following forest fires, other species begin to flourish. Whatever type of tree is progressive, but does not exceed its own resources, becomes a healthy one. A relaxation starts to come into a group following upheavals, there is an overwhelming evidence of long stable, even dull periods of time in between, in whatever group you may describe. The very functional becomes the very stable.

The internet itself is an amalgamated medium, a group, always progressing, always influencing itself. The available information held within its many convoluted spaces is an analogy of natural systems and the value in what is adopted over time.

"Meaning doesn't come from data alone. Creative problem solving depends on context, interrelationships, and experience. The surrounding matrix may be more important than the individual lumps of information"

Clifford Stoll

All possible transformations can eventually find their way into the overall architecture of a body. As structure relates to representations and a history of alterations the tree and the brain do in fact become more alike. A long-term mixture of shake & stop is very important in how transformations in animals will grow into capacities. An active reminder of why we possess so many dormant genes. This is incorporated into the networks of survival over the distance of time. Groups of networks employ timing as well as physical sophistication in order to create reactions that can help make the most of circumstances. These re activities are just how our tree has used dirt, sun and water, along with proper timing and countless other factors in order to become autonomous and adequate. The consistent habits are used to change a systems balance, it is the process with which it moves forward that is most important.

The Message of Ants

Really natural behaviours perform better in groups. So it has been social biology that has pointed out the actual expressions and mannerisms behind social creatures. With a slight coordination the overall benefits and the magnitude of options for a group increases. Relationships simply allow greater information processing, there is an inherent stability in distribution, when systems as wholes can progress in communications robustness is the result. One may not immediately realize it but actually with only "two percent of insect species (being) social, they (actually) represent more than half the insect biomass." (Levin, 1999) This is amongst those ants dwelling in forested regions. Their interrelatedness, their colonies

& their communications have led to their apparent success. The connected world becomes very valid in a hurry once aggregate transactions are now the functional rules. The beginnings of the agglomerate system, is within its tentative unions, as with the evolution of our tree, a forest itself is its network.

During the 1960's the French mathematician Rene Thom developed a beautiful conceptual idea, and named it Catastrophe Theory. He devised it as a way to illustrate the way in which overall systems switch between states of stability. It was discovered that even within many different surfaces nature had a way of shifting patterns, and then combining them within self-emanating structures (Lewin, 1999). It was to be a flow within an actual adaptation. In investigating the biologically complex he seemed to point out how things arrange themselves into pressure points. Upon this a divergence followed, leading to an inherent creativity during stable time & state periods. It is as if the speed of their adaptation became pushed towards the brink of total disturbance & into a position of greatest attainable fitness. As if an actual location, it became where each possible specialization materialized into a real and relative advantage in coevolving systems. Here characteristics and unique properties took root, it has been evident that too much creativity can actually hyperextend a system.

As with the developing human world, much of the indicative pattern also rears its head. Collapse usually follows a flurry of building activity, as if a desparative motion to avoid the stress put unto them by natural causes. The archeologist Joseph Tainter whom pointed out this aggressiveness, showing their actions carried out by the colonies themselves. Architecturally this is a formation, a self-organization and a behavior, put on by a collective mass of individuals as they form complex societies. Rene Thom merely suggested a ceiling in their temporary fit.

Our Biological Limits

Our tree formation is subject to physical restraint, for it cannot simply go out into its surroundings and get resources, the speed at which pieces come together are based in what comes to it. A geometrical assembling has much to do with necessary connections, those by which create function and efficiency. Patterns arise when things begin to diffuse together, making original combinations, making new stabilities and relationships along the way. How these come about has long been the study of what is thermodynamics, along the lines of how each physical property is generated. The collection of reactions throughout the entire construction of a network comes about from novel combinations of what factors make differences, as little pieces fit in with the bigger balance. We can observe repetition of form once these actions are established. In something known as ocular dominance stripes, those found in animal coats and ripples in sand dunes, we have a connection to chemical and biological systems. These are known as Belousov-Zhabotinshy reactions (Lewin, 1999). Their makeup is due to some simple characteristics, a similarity in overall form, the speed of the formations and their high dependency on aggressiveness of the reactive parts. With a quick look into the behaviour of such a process, the conclusions themselves lead us to self-similarity & the limits of form.

Diversity is a major benefit, recording of what went right and managing qualitative influences, in the way that patterns lend themselves to the influence of an overall architecture. The time it takes to perform some behaviour will over time lessen, and the success will establish itself as a pattern, slowly solidifying. As shapes form within shapes, complexity builds & slowly progressing equilibriums usually quicken, as this increases a critical geometry arises.

The build-up, as groups of local actions can release big changes is known as a type of determinism. A manifestation of pressures can eventually affect the entire populace of a network, causing the whole of itself to change. When things add up, behaviour is born out of the individual elements and within their relationships to one another. This is the basis of a collective agency, one which acts in connection of local and whole basically at the same time. The number of connections far outweighs the number of agents and individuals make up the whole. An idea of the complexity of this type of body is absolutely complex, with a mere 100,000 variations a possible $10^{30,000}$ possible states of action exist. This is the root of behaviour in things such as proteins and organic bodies. Actions then become a purely deterministic thing, for we know organization exists over absolute randomness. Real repetition does happen, but as with games like chess we do see its rarity. In that immense type of complex system, usually only 300 states are settled upon, this is a behavioural type of thing (Stuart Kauffman).

Information itself becomes a function of the whole, all pieces considered part of the fabric are part of its transfer. Considering qualitative changes as groups or clusters of things grow, usually within some manner of stability, gives us descriptions of actual influence as this information is carried through time.

The very exquisite delivery of instructions, whether on the level of the protein or in populations of ants, the reactions and evolutions of a system, leaves us with a firm sense that information is in fact qualitative. The time it takes for groups to exhibit behaviour is only related to what the function of that behaviour is, what purpose does it serve, and which individuals are causing and receiving its influence.

Together clusters in both the natural and man made worlds are directive, in that they do not simply wander out of control, but are brought from the brink of change through complex arrangement in what has taken place before-hand. The actual timeline of growth and influence carries with it future consequences, of which must be hampered or dealt with by the overall body as it copes with changes and rearrangement in its surroundings. To grow is to integrate, and to succeed is over enough time, being able to overcome catastrophe and suddenness. Likening the manner in which sequoia trees became fire resistant. These items being visible, it is always a position of time as to how many upheavals a group has surmounted to remain a cohesive healthy unit. The sheer mass of possible interconnections that constantly is attainable within an agglomeration is not constantly within reach, the scaling down of behaviours, a simplification of patterns, is an actual thing that does happen. It is what is found in nature. What are the most influential patterns to take, and where is a group going? This is determinism & the evidence suggests a collective is always going to become well organized.

Chapter Sixteen-
The Geometrics of Learning & Propagation

What lends itself to make good mistakes outnumber bad mistakes? With the brain, an instrument and ecology of its very own, with a highly select means of overcoming problems, it is hard to use simplified descriptions of how this works. Standing for or against certain kinds of outside influence, using neural groups the brain does piece together connections. Location is a factor, with different types busy with different exchanges, considerable reactions take place within neural relationships. A sharing of a placement and purpose leads to a history within the brain, of different memories.

Per Bak, Chao Tang & Kurt Weisenfeld began doing something different in 1987, they started playing a kind of game, one that involved patience. In this they began putting individual grains of sand one onto another, slowly, just to see what would happen. At first it revealed very little and then after some time they were witness to a sort of quirk. Perhaps it came out of sheer oddness as a somewhat peculiar waste of time showed a very unpeculiar result. Each time a layer of sand became stacked upon a previous layer of sand a linking network became visible, as if just holding onto the surface of the pile itself. Here was a strength, a structural one, as if bones holding the burden against gravity, a layer housed a stable mat. But after each adding of another and yet another grain came severe pressures to maintain, but eventually something happened. It was a cataclysm. Each web of sand crashed, and as links were spread throughout the skin of sand, all the grain were affected immediately, the sand came down the pile very fast. This is the action of a distributed network, and even though it was just bits of sediment, it was rich with organization and inherent information as to how it came to such stabilities in time. These three men are well known in the world as theoretical physicists.

In a series of events there became a network of reliance. One with which a discrete type of organization loaded itself into the fabric of these connections, one where the movements amongst them had the potential to make big changes. The brain itself operates under this style of influence, this same precise nature. Factions placed on the edge of influence, relationships with the potential to affect one another at any time. In a laboratory sense it is named the 'rise of factions', and those stable states that cause normality are associated with their everyday life. With the many ways with which a piece of the puzzle can embed itself really does come a relationship to the unpredictable results it may cause, it is in fact architectural. The shapes that are temporary and yet part of the function of a group are behavioural. They give the directions by which change will head off into a time of upheaval, those times when pressure is released. It is a manifestation within the behaviour of something physical as it relates to communication. The biology of groups operates in these same clusters, sections of the passing, of exchanges, working according to the same root. Thresholds have become part of our understanding of the brain and information theories. These complex arrangements, actually their consequential molecular arrangement applies to the synapse itself, in a very real fashion. Cells are progressive, as is even cell death, and are important plays in the wholes of organisms. There actually is mass correlation, & mass coordination in the tissues of the organic, with a purpose in sharing. The arrangements of individual elements in any system become built in a relation to one another, sharing a burden of influence, a placement of communication. Pressures are always manifested then released, rearranging the stress, actual 'micro-evolutions'. The contents of new information sewn into each part of the larger puzzle, brings forward the health of a faction of individuals, and paradigms of communication with self.

The Medium & the Message

The curiosities of the brain, with its exotic details left over from leaps in history. This is development of a rich geometrical cognitive orientation, one made to handle lots of information. The links amongst pieces are malleable, while static & plastic at the same time physical. Progress is made by the brain, problem solving is its specialty, and in every sense of the word, it is self-adapting.

> *"the quantity of structure incorporated into an animal's functional system is matched to what is needed: enough but not too much"*

Ewald R. Weibel

The blueprints of brain are generally the same with whatever kind of animal one looks at. Factions of neurons contain stabilized and active memories based on knowing, based on experience. Connections form into loops of feedback, they are also known as auto-catalysts, and are found all over the natural world. Those factions are related to a history of incidences, their configurations on capacity. The quality of the structure pertains to its function and what type of gaps appear, between what it is doing and what it needs to do.

It is a cluster, and a well maintained one, where electricity and chemical changes occur, bend and alter its contents and contexts, leading to biological and physical modifications & rearrangements and then, behaviour. As such it is a group, and has the actions and results that all agglomerations are subject to. When massive numbers of interconnectivity are present, in a system there are some things that tend to occur. Networks do work themselves into modes of action, patterns of activity where a state is stable. Then change occurs & the mode of activity switches to another, this is the fractioning which relates to the modes themselves, thus 'mode-fractioning'. The building & dissipation of stable states, of processes, of information, of thinking, of action is a common mannerism in natural groups. The interactivity, the plasticity and the adaptation all work in unison to make a brain function well. Seemingly 'steps' of action occur when learning takes place, over time the arrangements snowball their connectivity and then release their arrangement. In what can be referred to as a *recombination curve*, the long slow rise to a network of connections gives way suddenly to a reset, to a new state or mode of activity, where the rise starts again. This is an active pattern found in Electroencephalogram data, even earthquake data. The peak and fall is a qualitative aspect of groups where connections *are* the activity. Social behaviour, economies, growth of societies, mob behaviour, populations, weather patterns, structural collapses and countless other agglomerations exhibit this pattern.

Figure 4: Recombination Curve

It is a leap of faith to think of order as a normal mannerism in groups, this isn't the case for it is simply too complex for groups to have equilibrium. Our brains work well with pattern, & pockets of information stored in larger nests of related things, emotive, sensory or factual, the info is all somewhere between immediate and long forgotten.

Our abilities as people to understand the world around us and deal with surmounting piles of info everyday is overcome by a novel ability to *recombinate*, one found anywhere we choose to look in the natural world. Handling what matters, what doesn't, and all in between, is what makes us particularly ourselves. We must manage ourselves without being overwhelmed, and whatever these activities are they seem to work very well. Both sociology & psychology are tuned to conceptualize much of the goings on with both groups and individuals. There is a lot to know and the specifics themselves are always explorative in their nature as to how groups of things work. But as it turns out, biology has much to say about this.

Chapter Seventeen-
The Nature of Information

> *"Eventually, everything we currently believe will be revised. What we believe, then, is necessarily untrue. We can only believe in things that are not the truth...I think"*

Max Guyll

Methods

The established theoretical methods of how we view life itself, will inevitably change. If we are an investigative population and care to further our own knowledge then we must choose to progress down one avenue or another in this pursuit. What remains unexplored is vast and quite unique in perspectives, which still deserve our considerations. The very nature of 'progress' actually becomes difficult to nail down, progress just for what & for whom. A holistic view of the world, those held perhaps only in a few philosophical circles, has been fleeting from the more methodical ways of science. There are connections between eastern philosophy and many modern mathematical equates we have of our world. As quantitative and linear world swell and grow into such fluid patterns and behaviours en masse, in some nonlinear way we achieve a qualitative curve. There is substantial evidence that life itself can be seen with a qualitative consistency, rather than with a reductionary and mechanical determination. Across very diverging systems, that eek out an existence every day, is some sameness.

Patterns within the natural world do help with our own relations and hence our understanding of how things work. The popularity that exists with the social sciences, the overall study of the patterns they present, as well any qualitative consistencies of neuronal process like LTP, are to be understood as embedded. An explanation must include the relevancy of present relationships, rather than just a purely informational sense. The actual structures, those which are required for relationships to continue are within the design side of this talk & allow us to bring forth a world of associations. This neatly leaves behind the style of argument that seeks to ultimately define what *is* information, a semantic and difficult to diffuse term. Life is bound to happen despite what is defined correct, as information is not automatically so, but the relations will continue no matter how mutated things become. This can be a more applicable method for people in a general sense.

In a view of a social setting, one in which individuals share different perspectives but share conversation, there is always a bearing on how to relate. As if by way of a story, we have someone who is themselves unique, and living out part of their lives by working away in an occupation. As if establishing a story is of just a typical day in the life of this individual. Here we must see inside of what manner is usual for them, in that how they tend to their thoughts & what they pay attention to. There will lay certain characteristics both in and out of their usual way of performing tasks and in how they carry themselves along. As a relative-ness may be concerned, a social example may shed light on the adequacies of just what kind of information we are interested in. If we could take one such person, in one social setting and look into their habits, just what it is becomes useful & pertinent to them in their daily existence. Then we would have something.

A Gardener

In light of this, we choose a gardener, a realm easy to identify with. There are many details of and about this person's life, all of which will take time to expose. We have merely what we are told, directly, and aside from this we have visible characteristics. Of those items we can see as she plays out her daily routines, doing her work, some would be less obvious. Much can be known, but what is pertinent to us is what we keep our eyes open for, what will relate to us. Experience, both before-hand and as we are to see it, all relates to this unfolding of information. It helps us to identify what is going on and possibly will happen.

We can start with a description. It becomes her behaviour which we study, as we get to know her. What this person's life is like, with all their day to day tasks is very concrete. What their thoughts are unto an observer is quite abstract. The associations between the two are natural. The variety of characteristics we may discover about her is possibly informative, but is it information?

On a given day, we can see what our gardener does, moment to moment, we sit and watch her for a while. Over time we may become more aware of the way she moves, and the methods she employs, her thoughts however are hidden from us. She has a necessary relationship with her environment, she pays a lot of attention to the plants, as she is passionate about them. She has learned from her experience of working here, and much of what she does is self-relating and skillful. She also is coupled with a set of terms which allow her job to be specified. The knowledge pertaining to her horticulture and to her associates gives her a unique language. Her abilities to do the job at hand are personalized by habits, things we see she individualized with her interactions.

If she is to speak with her boss on some details of the work she is doing, there will be some goal in mind, something she will no doubt understand. In their language there is some efficiency, a series of informative structures which constantly make things easier and more focused. Beautiful things are shaped by the hands of these people and style & actions are built into any communication.

Vision of aesthetics is what it is they are hoping to accomplish each and everyday at work and to deliver on their job through information and action. Human nature provides associations with just the way this is achieved, and what it looks like to us. Much of the technical jargon of the job is invisible to us but we do understand what they are more or less doing as they toil away at their jobs. Is there truth? Is there absolute information in this occupation, perhaps not, but it is more than likely not a central concern to a gardener, as they perceive just how to do.

A Draftsman

The way things are supposed to look, a world of design and technical jargon, rich with the outcomes and physical landscape for society. All of the building up of the places we live in and the tools we use come down to plans. The language of the engineering and design world is vast & pertains to a great deal of details and motions. Harnessing all these specifics has been the achievement of many years of effort and focus of the dialect itself. Putting all of this down on paper is the job of the draftsman, and it must be done to perfection. How people will be able to interact with the final product of all these layers of information all comes down to the ability to keep it well organized and understandable.

Carrying out the direction of a plan is a great effort, from conceptual design to the lifespan of perhaps a museum or even a pair of shoes, and is the science and the art of making things functional as well as appealing. With any design in mind, the drafter must set out to capture the larger & smaller picture, and bring it clearly into view. A set of plans must contain an accessibility whereby any other understanding of its symbols and terms will be easy to read. Scales of information are very central to the universality of the information contained in a set of blueprints, and this graphical language is to be mastered in order to best communicate.

The language is the functionality, and the idea surface by which action follows, as in art of almost any kind. The transference of individual packages of information, and just how they relate and tie-in to one another, becomes the intelligence of the syntax itself. Technicality relating to an aesthetic of the overall product, made by someone for someone, requires visualization of the final form. How the series of events takes place along this timeline to best fit and most accurately capture what is being made is a rather long process. In the capacity of being skilled with

154

the process it usually requires a fair amount of learning to gain the tools of communication firstly, and then the capacity of artistry secondly.

An individual with a different occupation and set of lingo, mannerisms and style of work, but equally able to communicate ideas may not be able to read the plans. Across any other method of piecing a picture together, such as with a painter, there are differing sets of associations, the way information is met with action. Unto this our drafter is unique, like the gardener, and has yet no less of a task when setting out to capture what the structures and public places are that we would like to share within our cities, the overall vision of the places we live and the ways that we shape them into existence becomes a manifested and necessary occupation, just like the gardener. Our experiences with the forms of building and park alike, bare impression on our very own lifestyle & thoughts, and this is part of the spectrum of consideration that we invest into places like museums. If we are to witness this process as the drafter applies his curves and lines to paper, we could capture some methods of just how this individual goes through the motions in achieving this end. In a small sense the behaviour of the individual helps mold the process to his personality, and the association made within the graphic language will come to be through his characteristic of work.

Still amongst the larger picture of our world, how much universality lies within the information put down on these specific pieces of paper? With what command could these pieces of paper tell us anything about the rest of our world. Well not that much in a general sense of how things work, but maybe due to how much the associations are specified

155

to what the need is for them. But that does not diminish our ability as the viewer to understand the integrity of the final work, the visual aspects of the outcome, as no less are we taken by the form which the gardener has presented. In our capacity as everyday people to pick up on the character of both the final embodiment of work as well as the behaviours of those persons who made them, we are sharing in the literacy and meaning of the form itself. How we fit together this language is part of the ground layer of our ability to naturally associate with one another and take part in what each other is doing.

A Lawyer

Amongst those who place an imprint on our lives as well as shape the avenues by which we live our lives are in the sense the makers of how we are to abide by rules. In a profession with determined vocabulary, rules and methods of following through procedures, the result is no less concrete than the artist. Although in very different environments than a gardener or a draftsman, there is still a common language of making things and doing things and sharing ideas. Any methodology will be quite unique from any other occupation, a legal servant has many lesser known aspects and terms than most others. More along the social measurement of our societies and the individual play of citizens, the lawyer is a type of architect within the overall function of groups and what is permissible in our communities. Association of justice to the relationships of people, as well as rights, our abilities in how we function day to day contains an influence for others, we learn from our guidelines of society.

As if by a more subtle aesthetic, the layers of what we can do as people, is the overall shape to our societies, and within that are the structures of our behaviours. How we observe the activities of the lawyer are at utmost distant, as much of their actions are hidden within the language with which they do their work. As with our gardener and our drafter, we can pick up on much more of what they are doing and relate to a more personal level the type of result they are working towards, a lawyer's actions are much more opaque. It doesn't make the outcomes any less valuable, but it does illustrate the language by which they are carrying out what is needed within their occupation, and the complexities therein.

This communication is by a result of what works best for their tasks at hand, and is a little less accessible and general than other jobs. The aim is to make a difference in how we view things in ourselves in our worlds. In our groups, within our mental aspirations & amongst the things we strive for, all our capacity to make things are shaped by our laws and guiding rules.

The City

The outcome of the methods and the associations of languages is the bigger picture. The knowledge that we are able to relay through the places in which we live is probably the most important outcome of our own learning. Our cities are the grand design and cap of all that we have learned as people.

As if a combination of these three different people, their ideas as to the best city for them to all coexist in, we can

157

measure a qualitative effort of technical language. How they are able to modify their surroundings, & how their city is a changing living place they all must contribute to. It is the tie that binds them, as they all live close to one another at least indirectly, what is their shared perspective of architecture, or green spaces, or best guidelines. Social means set into design, form and behaviour becomes sociology transferred into our surroundings. It works as a basic visualization, a manifestation of how things should be put together in formal manner, to best suit the users of a city. How the individual pieces of the puzzle are slowly brought into alignment is the actual trade, and by many specific methodologies, we have made permanent inroads into how to actually do the work best.

When each of these 3 individuals comes to work the place their impressions of what the communication shall be from what it is they are working on, a great piece will make great reactions. In many ways it is the sharing of knowledge, the finalized product of what has been gleaned from lessons. Referring to the structures where we spend most of our time indoors, they affect our moods, our thoughts and our aspirations, all based on ambience. Great architecture is the showpiece of our competence within the natural world, and a disciplined artistry. If we think about our gardens we realize our imagination is at work, we find solitude, tolerance and reflection within spaces of beauty and natural ebb & flow. The gardener has played with a certain type of control, one bearing influence on our own possibilities in life. If nothing more than a way to enjoy a sun filled day, a garden is always appreciated & adored. The Venitians placed much confidence in the public spaces, and at the end of the day gained a lot from them, places to learn, places to build whatever comes next. The subtle transfer of knowledge is so indirect and so unusual, it takes the learning of patience and the developing of an eye for what one is actually viewing. Getting to know the subject matter may take years, great architects have often buried many secrets in their final designs, many of which take decades to discover.

Putting things together is the culmination of many teachers and fine attention of many students. To have an art form be legible to any one person who pleases to view it is because the association of languages had not become over laden by the technical. Information in a defined sense takes a secondary role for what is pertinent within a design or social setting, true formalized information fails to exist within a world of senses. Personal experience does not fit absolute description, but becomes a sophisticated emotive gathering of personal histories. The creation of these relationships with our surroundings, is our way of dealing with the present and or perceptions of events as they happen, or of what we think they may be. By this, art & information are really not the same thing.

Relevancy & Adaptation

Has relevancy been seen before in the natural world? By this, does it make anything somehow more real? In any sense we must lean towards the answer of yes. A qualitative process inside of any one way of doing things would make something 'like' itself. In the living world, self-referring structures are known to exist everywhere, one type is the catalytic reaction. Where things act in groups and must rely on some type of organization, there is an essential role to be consistent according to something else. Metabolic cycles, as they are mainly composed of chemicals, are described as cognitive and self-like (Capra, 1996). Loops themselves do contain pertinent information about the outside world, but mainly are built according to what works well within it. They do have stored characteristics and actually do interact with other living structures, just in sustaining themselves. The relevancy is about what is important at what moments in time. Bacterial cells and neural cells alike are physically reforming themselves to be part of a whole. When one aspect alters, it chains effects for others, constantly & must be measured.

Organic structures allow function and maintenance on a continual basis simply because cells and tissues are always in flux. This is an organization where the structure dictates the behaviours & relationships in the biological process (Capra, 1996). These actual components of the organization are embodied & each characteristic of the forms themselves are due to the patterns of assembly and function.

Any constant interaction with the surrounding environment develops into a series of associations, measurements even neurons are capable of controlling. The process of interactivity, and modifying one's own actions based on changes, creates cognition. A great many stimuli are important and many others are not unto a group of neurons, it pertains to their relationship. Whereby a vast number of random signals can be selected from and result in a networked and planned response, giving a variation to behaviour as well as to the character of an organism. It is the responses in their great variation which become complex, and each does have a connection to cognitive operations. There is communication, there is coordination, across many groups of cells and develops into organized and purposeful behavior, internal associations from external realities shape the structure of the living being. There are no truly independent existing worlds, as all have mutual coupling, either directly of indirectly. Information is not readily-made and pre-existing in the world, it is to be extracted by each cognitive system (Fransisco Varela). These complex associations instead are more descriptive and accurate as to what things actually become, a richness of informative things.

"You don't think of numbers when you listen to music or the intricacy of structure when you're in space, but you respond in an almost visceral way to music and architecture. Both of them are very precise, controlled and probably the most disciplined of all fields."

Daniel Libeskind

Chapter Eighteen-
Control Architecture in Nature

A Simple Situation

In formations of all kinds there is control architecture. By this the acting agents, composing multi-agent systems, share determinants of each other's activities, these coordinate and then emerge as global behaviour. Control architecture is the physical makeup that contains the capacity to share the most simplistic of influences. With the formations come the ability for coordination of intelligent problem solving (cognitive) behaviour, it depends on the associations present within a group, and it depends on how they may change.

The Geometrical Network is Inherently Reactionary

If someone were to begin building a model, one that was a cluster of inter-related parts, and the many links between each piece as if strings between lego© pieces, then it would take only a change or two for something to emerge. A composure of a group quickly becomes established, local efficiency prevails. At first the connections of individual elements was very casual, then after establishment of some efficiency, there is a formal establishment of lines. In a simple mathematical trick a behaviour can be found with "the number of links divided by the number of nodes (i.e. the ratio) approaches 2, a cluster, or the whole network undergoes such a phase change" (Bonabeau, 2002). By adding to the connections even a little we a huge impact on the actual size of the group, and establish order, and the ways things function and develop within the group evolves very quickly.

There are critical aspects in these groups, just how embedded certain pieces are, relates to the number of outgoing connections. Whether a species within an ecosystem, or a network of neural ganglion, a node is important due to the sheer number of outgoing connections that influence the system. An element whose state of function is less pertinent is if its relationships are composed of mainly incoming links, but if one provides enough stability it becomes a keystone type. They are few and far between, perhaps 1% or less, but when removed causes all sorts of havoc and collapse. This is not meaning that naturally they are never rooted out, and the strength they bear not eventually useless, in fact it is rather constant (Bonabeau, 2002). The number of outgoing and incoming influences, the feedback communication, signals or tends to create patterns that are highly adapted into the smaller of the worlds, which still must relate to the whole.

Coupling

Establishment of the specifics found within networks is easily explained. A characteristic and a dynamic are based on each individual amongst the links of the whole. The actual patterns of structure can teach us of behavioural attributes, those lines that are orientated to shorten distances within the web like pattern in a network allow individual elements to possess more specific importance. Circumstances of support can be attributed to any one node, and these specific adaptations for position are more specialized. More and more locally effective groups, actual clusters of elements give advantage for fewer movements are needed to exchange communication. Among elements, neighbours are given direct access, this is known as degrees of separation and there is some logic to its architectural structures for it becomes "possible to sort nodes in terms...so that individuals appearing at the periphery tend to be isolated" (Bonabeau, 2002). This influence allows complex behaviour at the local level.

While watching termites build nests, an epistemologist named P.P. Grasse (1959) came up with a rather potent idea. As the activity went along in front of him he noticed larger pattern bourn indirectly from smaller activities, this became known as stigmergy. Actions become based entirely on previous actions were the mannerisms making complex construction possible, these referred to as effectors. The most likely case in what he observed was that as the bugs moved around smaller balls of mud marked by pheromones, and eventually a larger shape came into being. Each contributing placement was in addition to all previous combinations in an elaborate ballet of community. In what could easily have been some random movement, a proximity to other balls of mud, each having a marker allows any deposits begin to form patterns. It is a chemical blueprint that functions external to the participants, orientation makes "columns to be built with a bias towards neighbouring columns, and eventually the tops meet to form one arch, the basic building units"(Franklin, 2002). There wasn't any direct relay of information, it was all done by trace chemical signals amongst the players, it is all done by sense. Local goals and a concentration on clumps resulted in controlled design, an architecture with intelligence. It is done by acts (traces) and the results of those signals (reactions), formed into a behavioural pattern (coordination) and then a physical one (columns).

This is a collective agency at work, an agglomerate pool of activity with a purpose. There is a process of each individual and a group measurement of their environments, something known as a cue, combinations of actions, bringing about larger results in rather seamless style, "coordination emerges incidentally" (Franklin, 2002). Even proteins can be organized using magnetism.

Combination Architecture

In our life and as individuals, we must cover the gaps that challenge us in our survival, we must solve many novel problems. In this capacity it has become known that absolute replication is not very successful. Distributing the risks and choosing from variations seems to carry a much more positive result. Even in the composition of antibodies in "the immune system blocks of DNA-and joints between them-are selected at random by microscopic chemical processes"(Stephen Wolfram). Novel combinations, even on the level of the small, form powerful and varied yet stable possibilities. Originality, physically, is the ultimate tool. In cells and even in chromosomes it is borne out of chemical interactions, in people, plants & animals it is made from mutual activities. When a body of the materials, which compose us, forms out of singular components we are still requiring a style, a phenotype. This is in what unions are the usual for an evolutionary gain. We are looking at collective process, the manner of coordination along the lines of basic experimentation. Influence spawns creativity, it is a very environmentally based action. This interactivity is archetypical, and perhaps plays a major role in the final form. The end results of our own inventiveness does become profound, and is made out of elementary chemical & social building blocks, made to fit together in new & maneuverable ways. From even the tiny things that bother us as groups of individuals, or like cells in tissue, we come up with considerations that lead to sweeping changes in our abilities to cope with our world.

Our architecture, our writings our cultural values, our thinking all secrete evidence of what we have picked up along the way, as we attempt to improve our situations.

"it is from accidental things that originality arises"

Jean Miro

Biodesign

Having the ability to bring about selective result, to change one's own capacity within an environment, is clear result of both study & sensitivity. Many living families of organisms have great success stories, the positive result after accommodation of traits from the world around them, granting advantage. Temperature is one such thing, many times an issue in the survive ability of groups of busy plants or animals and in many cases it is the heat. Termites in the perfecting of home, the mound, have adopted curves and made it a science as to the ideal form of their nest, just as with maintaining inside comfort. To them the outside environment undergoes a daily fluctuation, in such an amount of posing some problems, and so they devised climate control. Due to the shape in the curve of the shell of their mud houses they have been able to keep the temperature steady over a 24 hour cycle.

Physical attributes relate mechanisms & structures to functionality, and in many cases this comes with an aesthetic typology. It seems inspiring the way highly durable natural materials can be the result of adaptation, the careful molding of environmental aspects into the ideal, the basis of architecture itself. Photosynthesis is as much about the visual result of outstanding cleverness as it is of the efficiency and intelligence that went into making it happen. Constructively the supporting elements going into the makeup of a tree is just as striking. Materials put into physical attributes such as branching, where nodes thicken to give strength around joints & further function to reduce the torque placed on itself, there exist a strange amount of physics and engineering. Cantilevers that merge with supporting columns, like branches to a tree trunk, allow foundations such as root structures to carry more and further dissipate load, environmental & self.

Bio architecture suits that nature is the best designer, an optimization of patterns. There exist math centric shapes such as the seashell that contain the known "golden ratio" of maximization. Many of the characteristics attained from this have gone into manmade forms, such as the Parthenon. Its inspiration has made its way into much more abstract arts such as poetry, as in both rhymes and meters. Even in the musical world much has been made about form. Rather famously were the attunements of composition as with several of Mozart's sonatas & with Beethoven's 5th symphony.

Physical influence, such as with geometry and Feng Shui, exist in practice, further pushing the functionality of architecture and its ability to provide the physically positive.

Creativity is a source as well as a destination of producing things and ideas, it is a sign of health and fitness as well as of overall change and the passage of time. The act of moving mentally away from the rigid, from the static is a very necessary part of life, we must communicate and act, it is human behaviour. It can be common, it can be unusual, acceptable, irrelevant, useless, or even profound, but it all gets tried eventually. We do this using social norms, a means of control, the way we direct ourselves is thus a most basic human action. Comparative psychology, behavioural ecology, even socialbiology all concern themselves with the ideosyncracies of this process, but one thing is certain, behaviour changes over time. We are also what we breathe into things. As we piece it together we something, a diagnosis of the self, of our collective selves. Our groups and its family of parent ideas, help shape us. Looking back at us are the things we've made, they mould us, they are full with our own creations. It relates back, its an anatomy.

There are connections made in the experience as well, a fibre of externalized welds, this is biographical sensations, visual, spatial, audio... the linking of the space to overall surroundings, with communication, and the public. Add to it our capacity to fill it, to interact with in, to change with it according to our needs and what we intend to get out of it.

The similarity of self, even in architectural form is like memory. Form is a means of travel across time, it is a means of storage, it is some type of evolution, one opposed to rigidity & more like biological connectivity.

Afterword: the Art + the Personality

Art & Identity

Open space allows room for recombining pieces of memory into something novel, this applies to public spaces as well. Open areas give rise to free thinking and perhaps gives meaning to architecture. Actual experience taken from places can be said to influence our thoughts and perhaps our recall of memories. Can we nurture similar ways in which we can express the details within our memories as we set out to design our human places all around us? Artistic creativity embarks on filling spaces with meaning, representation, alteration, forming a graphical or visual relationship. Art, time, fitting of society as well as historical eras all match portions of these thoughts, as if by genre.

How much of the content of our lives has the description of what we think as art? How much communication between artist & viewer establishes an actual set of behaviours for art itself? The form of a piece itself has a qualitative nature about it. There is an automatic relationship with the speed of our own behaviour or consideration & the images conjured up in our minds. Both patterns and aesthetics are part of the substance interpreted by us and relates to our experience with the subject as well as how we remember it. Jungian archetype shows us that much of the collective of thoughts are unconscious and most often background to what we are aware of at the time of experience. Any remembering comes as a complex syncronicity, bound together with our own self-knowledge, self-order and self-adaptation.

The historical figure Osiris lent his teachings to archetypum, or the first molded. Lending our study to the beginnings of cycles themselves, how patterns took root. Perhaps along the same lines, Plato examined the characteristics, which could be discerned from living things and their apparent mental forms. It was Carl Jung's idea to interpret these observations and clump things into groups of memories. Memories relate to groupings. Plato wrote, but rather as a substance, an abstract non-material manifestation of memory. This was included in his theory of forms. Thales (from Miletos) directed his attention to an evolving meaning behind objects, as they would possess a substance of its own, a form of spatial (outside of the world) and temporal (outside of time) where things could simple go on being. We have tried to classify and define the substance of memory, throughout history. How our sense is manifested within our experience has brought us large questions about ourselves. Humans simply recognize that much more than an object, art is abstraction out of a virtualization, out of something that was previously thought or felt. Our ability to remember includes us with aspects of continuation, one that reaches outside of our bodies and into our immediate surroundings.

Art Itself

Value in Architecture as well as imagination, comes from a creative presence and a visceral influence both from the image in front of us and our image of it, a perception. It is an involvement of the self. Memory gives us a communication, an interpretation, of something that is art, and gives us the experience of human characteristic.

As a society can we further define our artistic inspiration, our artistic evolution, our artistic conversation? Douglas Morton, made a living as a painter, a Canadian born artist who played with the edge of stability within his works. His realm was that of the interactive, the playfulness of the human eye & how we perceive movement. In much of what he put down onto canvas seemed to push us into seeing movement where none existed, things moved around the edges on the canvas. It is a perception making a conversation with the mind, using the fringes of what our senses are definitely sure of and what they are not. It is subtle and it is purposeful, giving his pieces a unique and dynamic relationship with people, something that is static and yet isn't. His painting were somehow alive as they dwelled upon the canvas, leaving us with a burning question, how much of what we know is external from ourselves and outside of our own skin?

Memories in a pure sensory form, have an almost time-free existence about them. Whereas factual details of theory seem to fade after the passing of time, dismantled quickly by the everyday, our memories of our experiences linger, often as if they happened only yesterday. As a pictorial language, even with graphical interaction, there is a relationship to memory, we are each bias in the memories we hold. These help to shape the accessibility of all the contents of experience. Mood or emotional ambience that was present and helped to shape what actual events, seem to better grip our memory, at least more commonly, than any vast list of details surrounding the situation itself, we often carry a feeling and a few visuals about experiences.

Our own behaviour is etched into this making process. We may better relate to our attachments of memory and our sensations are malleable and remain consistent due to emotions. The placing of items into memory, pieces of a layered process involving senses, details, meaning, patterns, particularities, frozen moments, emotions as pre-existing knowledge, is a poorly understood occurrence, and a wonder of biology itself.

The things that art can help us visualize about being ourselves, is truly like a mirror, exposing things hidden in plain sight. Creativity as a source & as a destination of our own production of ideas, can and should be a sign of health, and proper changes in a person's own evolution and growth. Likely there is much to know about behavior when appreciating something artful, just as our impressions of objects is quite subjective, we respond an act to art.

Placement, realization, even deterioration of an attached memory all invoke the framing of how it was placed, but putting memories back into whole is supposed to be a function of the hippocampus. But as yet there is no explanation of the actual process of convergence, where fragmental aspects of a memory are put back together. By this there should be a distinction made between 'convergence' and the translation of the human mind.

Art Human

Memory as a process, tied to perceptions, is associated with form and the communication of the pictorial and auditory world. We make connections based biographically in the experience, by what we already think of ourselves within our surroundings. Our senses of sound, space and visualization are correlated with how our memories are made, interacting with our own actions, as well as our preconceived beliefs. With our attachments to our surroundings, as with architectural relationships, there is a self-similarity even in the sense of cultural norms. There is a structural rigidity to how things are done, and likely a bias to how things are remembered in this sense.

"an interior reality that expresses the spirit"

Jean Miro

Memory actually is self-influencing, a fluid like phenotype, a gravity of sorts, containing characteristic, conscious recollection as to what is usual. Both the texture of an experience and the meaning as it survives over spans of time have full influence on the individual. The amalgamation of these with previous experiences reflects the manner in which new things are absorbed into the overall change and growth of an individual and their personalities, their behaviour, their perspectives. Self-expression and experience exist in a pool of information and sensory history that leads to the present version of personality.

Art as Basics

Beauty, if simply aesthetic, versus order just by the basics is somewhere within the idea of functionalism. In with any

175

thoughts that if something holds a use, even if it looks good, it gets to be somewhere serving a purpose. The accommodation of something merely containing beauty is important to the value it holds, this is too a purpose as everyone is enriched by inspiration. The open ended-ness of, let's say artwork is a slow naturalism of a learning about our own human culture. Lovely things as well as completely functional objects hold the capacity to develop a meaning within our daily lives. This isn't a suggestion that all art serves in this way, as many pieces of art serve to shock and rely on absurd connections that do not establish themselves in any culture. The longevity of art is qualitative, such as is held in the beauty of a forest or stream, a functional value that can unfold and reveal its design over many critiques is ideal.

Architectural theory has a few fundamentals of its own, based in long term understanding. Within importance of its subject matter are the aspects of Design, Proportion, Distortion & Style. All concrete as well as abstract all at once. Plato himself argued that beauty is a sign of a higher order within the world we live.

Contemplative aspects of architecture, the detail, the form, the curve, where there had been none before, keep things from being boring. It lends to a sense of wonder, an intellectual buildup. Lasting impressions within our surroundings give back consistently in intrinsic value. When something is free from the ordinary it is appreciable in the simplest form of design, it then is similar to art.

People Art

"the sketchbook is clearly about work in progress,
it emphasizes that design is about process, not
just product "

Neil Challenger & Jacqueline Bowring

It was Alexander Kostellow who developed the notion of educating industrial designers to be prepared for social aspects of society. As a manner of developing mature and well-rounded graduates for the Pratt Institute he strove to include historically relevant content that allowed designers to make well situated decisions in their work. This is a perspective of design knowledge, a consideration of philosophy as much as market-place.

Developing things which suit people requires knowing history and even much about the human psychology of intangibles. Pulling something right out of the air & then working out how to make it physical is where the seeds of true design lie. It is of what it takes to make things we can use. This is the world of question and imagination with design as an action, to make something possible. It has been this way since people have been around.

Difficulty is ever-present in taking first attempts at obstacles. Much of the manner is in taking the first cracks at it, in brave first swipes. Often getting something started is the most stubborn part. It is built of asking the right questions and then proceeding from there, getting a toehold on the problem. This is of the human mind, with consideration of many intangible factors, totally hair brained concepts or opposite materials, all for the same purpose. It may require every angle you can conceive, and it takes a mind to get the ball rolling, and it often takes a brain to get the job finished. Stepping out is an almost organic idea, venturing out into a quiet world of being unsure, but knowing the answers lay out there, waiting to be discovered.

The 'napkin sketch' is a very well-known bearing on a problem, one that is perhaps as mythical as it is real. Everyone knows someone who has a story that began on a napkin, and in that sense it is tangible. It is the process that is cerebrally going on that is the heart of the storytelling, some almost etheric activity that is driving the pen upon the paper itself, this is what fascinates listeners. It is 'almost as if something lept right off the page', this is what people are talking about with these sorts of tales. It's a question of what is almost palpable, it as an action often laying within the history & collectivity of the drawer themselves. Sort of having an idea of where things were going, and an inkling on how to get there.

Did you ever have someone tell you it was okay not to know? Everything that is highly interesting tends to begin this way, in a place where objects are hidden from view.

fin.